Making Dance Special

Developing Dance in the Curriculum with
Pupils with Special Educational Needs

Melanie Peter

David Fulton Publishers
London

David Fulton Publishers Ltd
Ormond House, 26–27 Boswell Street, London WC1N 3JD

First published in Great Britain by David Fulton Publishers 1997

Note: The right of Melanie Peter to be identified as the author of this work
has been asserted by her in accordance with the Copyright, Designs and
Patents Act 1988.

Copyright © Melanie Peter 1997

British Library Cataloguing in Publication Data
A catalogue record for this book is available from the British Library

ISBN 1–85346–434–1

Typeset by Textype, Cambridge
Printed in Great Britain by BPC Books and Journals, Exeter

Contents

To my parents, Jean and Jack Peter

Acknowledgements

This book feels as if it has been a long time coming! I have been nurturing it for many years – ever since I had the good fortune as a PGCE student in the early 1980s to have Veronica Sherborne as a tutor. Her pioneering developmental creative movement programme exemplified an approach to teaching which addressed the needs of the whole person and empowered pupils to take increasing control and responsibility as active participants in the learning process. The development of pupils' communication, sociability and ability to think for themselves was regarded as integral to the whole proceedings. This was somewhat unusual at the time: special education in the post-Warnock era was heavily into directive, behavioural approaches, focused on tightly-defined individual teaching programmes.

Veronica Sherborne's work established for me the notion that it was possible to instil rigour without compromising the essential open-endedness that should characterise practice in the arts. Indeed, it demonstrated how accurate assessment and planning developmentally appropriate experiences within clearly defined boundaries paradoxically *enabled* pupils to be creative. It reinforced, too, the therapeutic value of the arts as an interactive teaching and learning style, and in affording pupils the opportunity to express themselves and communicate other than in a written form. Veronica's approach profoundly influenced my work subsequently and consolidated my belief in the power and importance of the arts for all.

I have since wanted to find ways to embed and extend Veronica Sherborne's work seamlessly into the well-established approach to dance in education, originally formulated by Rudolf Laban (Veronica herself was a protégée of his). In 1984–5, I was fortunate to work with Walli Meier at the Laban Centre in London, and greatly valued the opportunity to develop my practice further with such an inspirational practitioner. She demonstrated an approach to dance in special education which harnessed much of Veronica Sherborne's philosophy. I have subsequently sought to marry these strands in a way that is compatible with statutory curricular requirements. I hope that Veronica herself would have approved of my endeavours – sadly she died in 1990.

In more recent times, I have been able to refine a developmental approach to 'dance for all' in a range of educational settings. I am grateful for all the support and enthusiasm I have experienced from colleagues and pupils along the way. In particular, from those at Nine Acres School, London, and at The Hall School, Norwich (both for pupils with severe learning difficulties), and at Bawburgh Primary School in Norfolk. More recently, from fellow advisory colleagues within Norfolk LEA's Arts-in-Education Service, and associates at Norfolk and Norwich Community Dance (especially Sarah Coverdale). Also, from my colleagues in the Centre for the Study of Special Education, at Westminster College, Oxford.

A special mention is also due to all my friends at Musical Keys – a voluntary organisation based in Norwich for children with special needs, their parents, carers and families, for whom I have been running a weekly creative movement and dance group for several years now. Not only has this been enormously pleasurable and rewarding but it has also contributed another dimension to my work.

I wish also to thank all those who have supported me in the process of compiling this book. In particular, Jillian Tearoe, Paula Stubbs and Christine Cutting for their help with the tables and diagrams. Also my son Sam who, at eleven years old, has proved himself a most able illustrator – a special thank you for his contributions to chapters 3 and 4. I am delighted that the Principal of Westminster College, Oxford, Dr Richard Ralph, has written a Foreword to the book. Friends and colleagues have offered comments on the drafts – particular thanks are due to Derek Paice and Tom Hunt. Finally, once again, I am indebted to my family for all their patience and support. *Making Dance Special* is dedicated to my parents.

Foreword

In moving to Westminster College, Oxford from London Contemporary Dance School, where I had been Principal for seventeen years, I identified few familiar areas of teaching activity. I was therefore delighted to learn of the important mission of the Centre for the Study in Special Education and, within it, of Melanie Peter's work with dance.

The professional dancers and dance students with whom I was associated for so many years used to work in the community as part of their training. This could involve residencies in schools or youth centres, or working with artists like Wolfgang Stange leading groups with special needs of one kind or another. This latter option was always over-subscribed because the experience it afforded was so immediate and real – because it revealed something of the universality of dance and of the power of dance to transform.

My students were able to see hour by hour in the studio how readily young people from all backgrounds and abilities respond to and grow into the experience of using their bodies to express an artistic impulse and a feeling which is too deep or too raw for words. Through dance they are able to connect their energy with that of other people and with that of the forces in the world around them – even when they can relate in no other way. Dance, like nothing else, harmonises mind, body and spirit and reconciles the contradictions of our natures and of our world.

People with special needs of all kinds can respond in a miraculous way. I remember my own father, dying of Alzheimer's disease, loving to dance around the room, when in non-dance mode he could manage only a shuffling walk. It is well known that many people with Down's Syndrome can dance with rare grace; and my friend Steve Paxton, the inventor of contact improvisation, discovered how moving in pairs can unlock in blind people that power of spontaneous and fearless movement which their disability tends to inhibit and constrain in them.

   Dance has so much to offer to the young, and I commend Melanie Peter's brave attempt to describe ways of placing this most mysterious and all-embracing of the arts at the service of those whose needs are very particular and for whom a non-verbal art form articulating itself through the physical body which defines our common humanity is uniquely suited. I wish Melanie Peter, the Centre of which she is a part, her distinguished publisher – and this book – well.

Dr Richard Ralph
Principal
Westminster College, Oxford
May, 1997

Introduction

This book sets the foundations for educational dance in relation to pupils with wide-ranging learning needs. It takes seriously the notion of 'dance for all' and explores a developmental approach for taking movement into dance, with strategies to enable learners of all abilities to progress in the context of National Curriculum requirements. It is grounded in the work of Veronica Sherborne and dovetails her developmental creative movement programme with the framework for educational dance pioneered by Rudolf Laban. This forms a basis by which individual pupils' needs in dance may be identified and addressed, and their achievements recognised. It offers a non-threatening approach to dance education for the most challenged teacher and pupil! In short, it suggests how to set about 'Making Dance Special'.

Educational dance tends to suffer from misconceptions. Many generalist teachers grasping after some kind of security tend to resort solely to using broadcast material. There are those teachers, too, who will perhaps put on a dance tape and somehow hope for the best, in the well-intentioned belief that this is empowering the pupils to express themselves freely. There are also those teachers for whom 'dance' in schools tends to be synonymous with country dancing – apparently endorsed by references in the National Curriculum (DFE, 1995) to 'performing movements or patterns including some from existing dance traditions' (Key stage 1), and that pupils should be taught 'a number of dance forms from different times and places, including some traditional dances of the British Isles' (Key stage 2). All of these approaches may have their place in dance education but, in isolation, are far from the whole picture! *Making Dance Special* considers implications for planning for progression and continuity, and breadth and balance in dance work, for pupils of all abilities.

The notion of dance for people with special educational needs (SEN) can arouse mixed feelings. On the one hand, it is recognised by many as a potentially liberating experience, a powerful means for non-verbal expression and communication, and a basic entitlement. On the other hand, it is sometimes regarded as a potentially undignified and embarrassing experience both for dancer and viewer: that it is beyond the capabilities of many people with SEN to achieve the technical refinement and grace that would appear to characterise notions of prowess in dance presented in the media. It is all too easy to see limitations towards achievement in dance, rather than potential, when faced with certain individuals experiencing physical disabilities, involuntary movement, lack of co-ordination, difficulties in organising their behaviour, limited symbolic understanding, and so on. *Making Dance Special* faces the challenge head on, in the belief that learners of *all* abilities may find enjoyment and creative fulfilment and achievement in dance.

Besides, pupils with SEN may not be disadvantaged in dance, and may demonstrate considerable *ability* relative to other areas. However, there would appear to be no getting away from the fact that dance as an art form relies on the body as its medium, and that certain individuals would appear to be seriously disadvantaged in using their body as an expressive tool. Dance, though, is not just about *expression*; it also creates *impression*. Pupils should be encouraged to develop their *knowledge and understanding* of dance as a means for organising, ordering and communicating significant aspects of experience, as well as their ability to *perform* a range of increasingly complex or subtle movements. Just as important, then, is interpretation of movement – learning to read body language – and realising how movements may be combined and ordered to create meanings in dance. Certain pupils may reveal their abilities as potential choreographers and dance critics, even if their active participation or development of technical skill may be necessarily more limited.

Making Dance Special presents an approach to dance, whereby *all* may learn the language of dance and the potential of the art form for encapsulating and sharing aspects of experience. Most pupils, let alone those with SEN, will require programmes of work to be planned in small increments, taking account not only of their need for new challenges but also of their need to consolidate their abilities and understanding in familiar movement experiences. Many pupils may have patchy developmental profiles in various aspects of dance work: skills in performance, their ability to compose dance, and in their ability to appraise or appreciate the dance of others. *Making Dance Special* endeavours to address progress in all aspects of dance work, to support the prospective teacher of dance with groups with wide-ranging learning needs.

Chapter 1 sets the context for developing dance work in schools. It looks briefly at the evolution of dance education, including consideration of National Curriculum requirements for dance. It also discusses the value of dance in the curriculum, including links with other curriculum areas, with particular reference to the needs of pupils with a range of learning difficulties. Chapter 2 presents a framework for dance education that is compatible with statutory requirements. It addresses individual needs by considering not only the children's stage of physical development but also by identifying their natural starting-point for dance, through observation of *how* they move. Laban's analysis of the dynamics affecting quality of movement is considered, and the inter-relationship also of the other movement elements (the body, actions, use of space, and relationships). Together, these comprise a basic structure for developing children's understanding and use of the art form of dance.

In order to move expressively and creatively, fundamentally, children need to learn to organise their energy and to co-ordinate the body (Sherborne, 1990). The first aspect is developed in chapter 3. It is proposed that this is fostered through *relationship play*: learning to adjust one's strength in relation to other people (a 'people as apparatus' principle). The second major strand is explored in chapter 4: how to develop youngsters' body awareness and knowledge of possible ways of moving. Chapter 5 demonstrates how a developmental framework for movement (explored in chapters 3 and 4) dovetails with a framework for educational dance, and may provide the substance for dance lessons. The chapter presents a scheme of work to support planning for progression and continuity in pupils' understanding and use of the elements of dance. It identifies characterising features in the movement elements, across four stages of development; effectively, it breaks down the kind of progress one might expect through Key stages 1 and 2 and into Key stage 3 of the National Curriculum.

Chapter 6 deals with the specifics of planning for dance, with pointers for developing work from a range of stimuli. The chapter also presents an approach for teaching particular dance styles and traditions, including step patterns, to youngsters with wide-ranging learning needs. It includes consideration of how the potential contribution of professional dance may be harnessed for enhancing children's knowledge and understanding in their own dance work: how to intepret and analyse dance, and develop themes in their own work. Finally, chapter 7 looks at the teacher of dance and implications for ensuring quality in practice. It examines the role of the teacher, teaching strategies and notions of progression in dance as they affect teachers' expectations. It addresses issues of differentiating and assessing dance work to meet a range of needs within the context of the group. It also includes a section on 'trouble-shooting' – some golden rules for managing dance work with groups. There then follows an Appendix of lesson plans which illustrate appropriate planning across the Key stages, as well as how movement experiences may be differentiated, to meet a range of needs within a group.

The approach to dance presented in this book is intended to be accessible to generalist teachers working with pupils with a range of SEN. One common confusion needs clarifying: the distinction between 'movement' and 'dance'. Having trained with Veronica Sherborne, I was steeped early in the concept of 'movement' education: her work essentially explored basic movement experiences within a developmental programme. However, many would term Sherborne's work under the umbrella of 'dance'. It was at the Laban Centre, however, working with Walli Meier, that I began to formulate how Sherborne's work could be extended into 'dance' in its narrower sense. In the main, I stick to the simplistic distinction of 'dance', as being 'movements' combined in a sequence to create a repeatable pattern, often performed to a rhythmic or musical accompaniment. However, at times I do use 'movement' and 'dance' interchangeably, to avoid clumsiness in style.

As with the other arts, certainly through Key stages 1 and 2, one does not have to be specialist-trained to teach dance successfully to children in schools, although one does need to be a good enabler. This begs knowledge of stages of development, and how to structure appropriate work in dance in order for children to progress. There exists relatively little on dance, in comparison with educational publishing in the other arts. I hope that this book will make a contribution to the dance education library, in offering teachers in mainstream as well as special education a developmental framework in which to extend their practice, to enable them to cater for wide-ranging individual needs....Small steps (pun totally intended!), in other words, towards 'Making Dance Special'!

CHAPTER 1

Dance in Context

Why dance? After all, it appears to be almost something of an afterthought in the eyes of the architects of the National Curriculum. Dance is not given the same discreet subject status as Art and Music, and has to share its place within Physical Education (PE) alongside timetabling demands of games, gymnastics, athletics, outdoor and adventurous activities and swimming. By Key stage 3, dance is no longer even compulsory. Perhaps we should be more positive! Let's look at it another way: *dance is now statutory for all children aged 5 to 11* (DFE 1995). This chapter sets the context for dance in the curriculum. It outlines the evolution of educational dance in schools and the importance of movement for child development. Its value within the curriculum is also considered, with particular reference to children with special educational needs (SEN).

Dance for all

Responding to life's rhythms appears to be an innate physical drive. Most of us will feel the urge to tap our foot along to the beat of some catchy tune. Witness, too, the steady rocking to some 'inner pulse' of certain disturbed residents in long-stay institutions: there is little doubt that movement gives a sense of solace and can be an integrating experience. Dance Movement Therapy (DMT) harnesses rhythm as a holding factor for some clients, and synchronous movement activity as a means to unite a group (Payne, 1992). In DMT, movement may be used to symbolise conflicts and give meaning to the inner world of those with learning difficulties and speech impairments: movement as communication in a more direct form.

Historically, there exists a vast range of traditions where meaning has been given to movement in order to express aspects of experience: ordered in rituals and ceremonies across cultures and in sequences of step patterns in dance. Different dance traditions have formalised their own respective structure, in order to create a shared language in movement. This may be highly complex, as in the hand movements of Javanese dancers. There has been interesting cross-fertilisation, too, of dance traditions to create new styles – for example, North American jazz evolved in the early part of the twentieth century, from the dance of exiled African slaves influenced by Western popular music. Many folk dances have their origins in the work or occupations of the particular culture concerned. As Lowden (1989) observed:

> The art form of dance is a way of forming and sharing the way we respond to the world in which we live by paying particular attention to experiences, and giving them significance, particularly those experiences that can be organised and ordered in bodily movement. (p. 4)

However, as with representational compared to abstract art, dance does not necessarily have to convey a narrative: meanings may also be created by the way the elements of dance (especially space, time and energy) are ordered for their own sake, perhaps to communicate emotions or feelings. For example, disco dancing involves specific actions, ordered in a particular way, and performed in considered relation to other dancers. Body language may be abstracted and stylised, and acquire significance within the bounds of the dance space: how the dancer moves in relation to other people, in relation to rhythmic or musical accompaniment, in relation to particular objects, or in relation to the floor, the dance surface itself.

Talent in dance is held in high regard across many cultures; in many advanced societies, there exist channels whereby youngsters showing particular ability or aptitude may have this nurtured from an early age: in dance classes or specialist schools, such as the Royal Ballet's school 'White Lodge', or in state-run provision as in Russia. Yet there is a sense too that dance is undervalued: some cultures historically have considered dance an expression of 'low life', even vulgar in comparison with high status arts such as music; for example, Medieval tumblers were effectively excommunicated.

All dance, essentially, gives *form* to movement, and therefore may be subjected to aesthetic judgement. Some achieve greater quality in movement than others, and bring this sensitivity to enhance technical excellence at executing steps, perhaps within a particular dance style. On that basis, it is often possible to recognise those who are 'good at dance', without necessarily fully understanding the significance of the particular body language of the tradition or dance style in question. As with art, a particular dance style may not always be one's 'cup of tea'. However, it is important to retain an open-minded attitude, and not impose one's own personal preferences or values on others – children, in particular, will be sensitive to picking up positive or negative signals from their teacher.

This raises the issue of the status of one dance style over another, which may be culturally relative. For example, is prowess in ballet more likely to be praised, as opposed to break-dancing? Are we able to appreciate subtlety in the dance of a relatively unfamiliar tradition? This would seem to emphasise the notion of appraising the dance *product* (the performance or execution), rather than the *process* of creating it (weeks of practising, perfecting and rehearsing perhaps). There is a sense, however, in which process and product in dance are necessarily always intertwined, fused even in final performance. So what is the relevance of all this to teaching dance to youngsters in schools?

Dance in schools

The notion of accessing 'dance for all' has its origins in the work of Rudolf Laban in the1930s. Laban first identified the *elements of movement*, which form the basis for modern educational dance to this day (see chapter 3). Laban's acclaimed movement observation and analysis was first applied in this country to the movement training of actors. His approach, publicised by his colleague, Lisa Ullmann, was subsequently developed in relation to the movement and dance of children. This was readily embraced by PE teachers, and the principles were also incorporated into educational gymnastics. Thus, historically, dance acquired recognition and status within the curriculum, and an early association with PE. Did this situation come about simply because dance was regarded as another physical activity that also involved the children having to get changed, and often moving freely within the same large space set aside for PE?

Controversially, perhaps, dance in the National Curriculum still features only as an aspect of PE, and is assessed as such by OFSTED (1994). Clearly there is a degree of overlap with development of objective physical skills, but these are harnessed in dance with a very different emphasis and purpose. As such, achievement should be judged in open-ended work, with expressive and communicative intent clearly in mind. Dance work should be subjected to the same aesthetic criteria as the other arts, such as music, art and also drama. There is no compulsion for dance to be solely the responsibility of the PE coordinator: in fact, in certain contexts, it may be more appropriately placed within the Creative Arts, provided that requirements are met.

So what is the value of dance in the curriculum? Is there something to be gained from participating in dance – engaging in the process – and sharing our endeavours with others, without the pressure of finesse in performance, yet nonetheless without compromising standards in achievement? One of Laban's and Ullmann's protégées, Veronica Sherborne (who likewise also started out as a PE specialist and physiotherapist), recognised the value of dance for meeting individual needs. In particular, she applied Laban's principles to institutionalised adults with learning difficulties, although she subsequently developed her work across the educational spectrum – in mainstream as well as in special education. Sherborne came to the conclusion that:

> ...all children have two basic movement needs: they need to feel at home in their bodies and so to gain body mastery, and they need to be able to form relationships. The fulfilment of these needs – relating to oneself and to other people – can be achieved through good movement teaching. (1990, p. v)

The legacy of all of these early pioneers in educational dance is an emphasis on the *development of the whole person through movement*. Compared to gymnastics, physical ability is of lesser consideration in educational dance. Rather, it is the way an individual lends subjective significance and meaning to movement in dance that is esteemed. The point is that movement work in educational dance is not competitive: it is not concerned with performing objective skills as an end in themselves. Rather, they are harnessed in dance education as a means to an end. However, this is not to imply that the development of children's physical skill is left as a matter of chance. It is the responsibility of teachers of dance to foster the development of their pupils' movement repertoire, from which they may then select and choose more purposefully and sensitively in order to create meanings in dance. Thus they may be enabled to order and lend significance to their movements, and learn that dance may have communicative impact. A case of 'learning how to do dance whilst doing it'!

Movement and child development

In considering the value of movement education, it will be apparent that a distinction can be made between the learning of functional motor skills and movement as an activity of the whole person. The former is related to practical need, in order to accomplish tasks more effectively and skilfully;

for example, the improvement of hand–eye coordination in ball games. In these types of activity the mind directs the movement. Valuable though this is, open-ended creative movement can contribute another dimension: it implies something more than physical activity. It involves the integration of intellectual, emotional and intuitive aspects of a person; in other words, movement *stimulating* activity of the mind. This, in itself, ought to provide justification for movement and dance education as holding a central place in the curriculum!

The relationship between movement and conceptual thought is widely acknowledged (Piaget, 1959; Cratty, 1975; Kephart, 1971; etc). More recent practioners (e.g. Nind and Hewitt, 1995) working with pre-verbal people with learning disabilities, have also re-emphasised the importance of movement experiences in developing communication, with a revaluing of 'rough-and-tumble' toddler-type interactions. By implication, Jordan and Powell (1995) would value the potential of movement and dance for developing a sense of 'experiencing self'. They uphold Hobson (1993), whereby affective engagement at a psychological level is considered critical for social and intellectual development: people with autism characteristically have difficulty categorising and relating to the world in relation to the self, and therefore in developing autobiographical memory and 'perceptually-anchored intersubjective communication'.

Veronica Sherborne (1990) highlighted the way movement education may have an important 'compensatory' function, offering the opportunity, in a sense, to 'recapture' early sensori-motor experiences. She contended that this is beneficial particularly (but not exclusively) to those for whom such experiences may have been limited (see chapter 3).

Several psychological theories of child development are rooted in motor activity. Kephart (1971) saw action as enhancing the child's body concept: the child learns to sit up, crawl and eventually walk as s/he is able to control and transfer weight, so that the body is the original frame of reference. According to Kephart, pure thought activities are based on the ability of the child to respond muscularly: through action, the child will gain crucial experiences to feed an awareness necessary for perceptual development; for example, laterality (left–right discrimination) fundamental to reading. The implication according to Kephart (1971) would be that motor improvement ought to allow for remediation of academic difficulties, which Kephart regarded as rooted in lack of early integration in perception and motor responses.

Cratty (1975) similarly attaches significance to the bonding of four development channels (verbal, cognitive, conceptual and motor). He maintains that at certain stages these 'imperative binds' must be connected;

for example, when a child starts walking. A disabled child therefore may be helped to make permanent bonds, to overcome his or her inability to integrate body parts when appropriate or to dissolve bonds or connections between motor abilities which are no longer needed together. This would suggest some fundamental implications educationally, if movement potential is impaired through neurophysical or cognitive dysfunction.

One of the most influential educational theories acknowledging the importance of movement is that of Piaget (1959): specifically, the contribution the active child makes to his/her own development. According to Piaget, all conceptual thought is rooted in a motor base: this gradually becomes superceded by internal representations of actions that the child makes to him/herself. Piaget identified four stages of cognitive modes of thought, through which a child passes sequentially, if not at precise chronological stages. Initially, the child learns to control reflexes and to act intentionally on the environment; make-believe and language emerge as the child becomes able to perform actions in the absence of objects. Gradually, the child becomes more decentred, and is able to sustain co-operative and social play, able to take the viewpoint of others, culminating in integration and then abstraction of thought.

The levels of functioning postulated by Piaget (1959) have been endorsed more recently by the work of the Froebel Early Education Project (Athey, 1990). In particular, children were observed to prefer operating within certain *schemas* – modes or patterns of thought and behaviour – which take on a developmental aspect as children mature. The implication is that there is an observed relation between children's action schemas and the development of conceptual thought into adulthood, and that children's preferred patterns should be nurtured. Children may be observed to prefer adopting certain movement patterns, indicative of their particular schema; arguably, then, these should be reinforced in movement experiences, as the sensori-motor underpinning to their subsequent development:

- dynamic-vertical (an interest in up-down trajectories – climbing, jumping, sliding, rolling)
- dynamic back and forth, or side to side (transporting, pushing and pulling along)
- dynamic circular (swirling, spinning, rotating actions)
- going over and under (exploring shapes, adapting body to space available)
- going round a boundary (moving in general space compared to personal space; elliptical pathways)
- enveloping and containing (negotiating enveloping spaces)
- going through a boundary (going through tunnels and enveloping spaces).

Piaget (1959) emphasised the importance of *active learning* through play: imitative play in order to understand an action, and symbolic play to consolidate that understanding in repeated activities. His theory has been very influential on curriculum design and delivery, particularly in Early Years education – for example, the High-Scope nursery curriculum (see Holimann and Weikart, 1995) is overtly based on children's active involvement in a 'plan-do-review' cycle. More recently in special education, such principles of *interactive* approaches to learning are being revalued. This is in the context of the emergence of the self-advocacy lobby within the disabled community, and the endorsement of active participation in the learning process. Also, interactive approaches to learning (Collis and Lacey, 1996), involving cognitive processing and positive action, are regaining favour over the behavioural approaches to learning popular in the 1980s (where learning was regarded as the result of practice and conditioning). Active learning also appears to be endorsed in many National Curriculum Programmes of Study, to which children of all abilities have an entitlement: for example, children are often required to 'explore', 'investigate', etc.

Besides, as Veronica Sherborne (1990) contended, many children with learning difficulties are 'stuck' at the sensori-motor phase developmentally, or else may need to 're-visit' it, in order to consolidate understandings (see chapter 3). Piaget's theory would appear to have the following implications for developing movement work in relation to the child's developmental level:

- the type of movement experience needed – opportunities to repeat and/or consolidate familiar skills, as well as to acquire and practise new movement possibilities;
- the type of relationship work possible – the extent to which a child is able to engage in partner work (with an adult first before a peer), before participating and negotiating with peers within increasingly larger groupings;
- the importance of play – movement and dance work as an enjoyable, unpressured experience, where everyone's achievements may be valued, without the fear of 'failure'.

Dance in the curriculum

Figure 1.1 summarises in table form, for easy reference, National Curriculum (DFE, 1995) requirements for dance across the Key stages. It will be seen that statements from National Curriculum Programmes of

Pupils should be taught . . .

KEY STAGE 1	KEY STAGE 2	KEY STAGE 3	KEY STAGE 4
(a) to develop control, coordination, balance, poise and elevation in the basic actions of travelling, jumping, turning, gesture and stillness;	(a) to compose and control their movements by varying shape, size, direction, level, speed, tension and continuity;	**Unit A** (a) to perform dances, showing control and sensitivity to the music and style of the dance;	(a) to compose and perform, accurately and expressively, increasingly complex and technically demanding dances that successfully communicate the artistic intention;
(b) to perform movements or patterns, including some from existing dance traditions;	(b) to perform a number of dance forms from different times and places, including some traditional dances of the British Isles;	(b) to perform dances, including set dances, from different traditions from the British Isles and elsewhere;	(b) to perform and create dances in a range of styles, showing understanding of form and content;
(c) to explore moods and feelings and to develop their response to music through dances, by using rhythmic responses and contrasts of speed, shape, direction and level.	(c) to express feelings, moods and ideas, to respond to music, and to create simple characters and narratives in response to a range of stimuli, through dance.	(c) to describe, analyse and interpret dances, recognising differences.	(c) to design and evaluate aspects of production for their own compositions;
		Unit B (d) to perform further dances, showing control and sensitivity to the music and the style of the dance;	(d) to evaluate aspects of dance, including choreography, performance, cultural and historical contexts and production.
		(e) to support their own dance compositions with descriptions of their intentions and outcomes;	
		(f) to describe, analyse and interpret dances, recognising aspects of production and cultural/historical contexts.	

Figure 1.1: National Curriculum requirements for dance

Study (POS) in dance are very broad and enabling; for example, no pupil, not even the most profoundly and mutiply learning disabled pupils, need be excluded from notionally '[exploring] moods and feelings and [developing] their response to music through dances...' (Key stage 1), or from '[performing] dances, including set dances, from different traditions' (Key stage 3) – even if they need support to do so. It remains the teacher's job to interpret and translate such all-embracing requirements into teaching objectives with observable outcomes, by which needs may be planned for and progress assessed. There is little guidance, however, to support teachers in their quest to address *how* this may be achieved.

Pointers relating to methodology in dance teaching have now been removed from National Curriculum documentation. From present guidelines (DFE 1995), it is hard to discern benchmarks for achievement in dance which may assist the teacher in planning appropriate work. Teachers of pupils with SEN may face an even harder challenge if their pupils' progress in absolute terms is relatively slow, often with irregular developmental movement profiles. Earlier National Curriculum documentation (DES 1992) indicated how *all* children need to progress in their understanding and awareness of the *elements of dance*:

- their use of the *body*,
- their ability to perform *actions*,
- their use of *space,*
- their use of contrasts in *dynamics,*
- their *relationships* to other dancers, to objects, to accompaniment, to the dance surface itself.

(Note that these elements will receive detailed consideration in chapter 2.)

However, unlike in Art and Music, specific reference to these elements of the art form of dance has now been largely removed from subsequent documentation: the elements of dance receive only passing mention, subsumed in the statements comprising the National Curriculum Programmes of Study (DFE 1995). This has left many teachers of dance seriously disadvantaged in approaching curriculum planning: as in Art and Music, planning in Dance should be driven by the need to deepen children's *skills, knowledge and understanding* of these very elements of the art form. As with other areas of the curriculum, teachers are liberated to draw on material from across the Key stages, to enable individual pupils to progress and demonstrate achievement, provided that this is presented in age-appropriate contexts. However, these exhortations have a hollow ring if the teacher does not have a grasp on how pupils may develop in the elements of dance.

Early National Curriculum documentation (1992) was unequivocal about emphasising pupils' *abilities* to improve their movement skills and to help change feelings of disaffection, under-achievement and low self-esteem. For example, a pupil with learning difficulties may be strong on performing movements in dance but relatively weak on planning or evaluating; a pupil with physical disability may perform at basic levels but show an aptitude for planning and evaluation. Working to pupils' strengths in this way may enable pupils to show achievement and progression in those strands which they can access most readily. Similarly, there was an important endorsement to interpret Programmes of Study (POS) freely and creatively; for example, 'travelling' to mean running/walking, but also moving in wheelchairs. Specifically, it was recognised that:

Dance provides an alternative means of expression for pupils to learn about themselves, others and the world around them. Dance activities can be modified to enable pupils who use aids to mobility to participate. The aid itself can be the focal part of the dance (DES, 1992, E5.5).

The contribution of dance and its *value to the whole curriculum* was also recognised in early National Curriculum documentation (DES, 1992), notably regarding:

- health education – fitness, warming-up and cooling down, posture, hygiene;
- matters of safety – especially good posture and correct use of the body;
- careers education – participation in dance vocationally or as a leisure pursuit;
- personal and social development – self-reliance, self-discipline, resourcefulness, co-operation with others, reappraising personal attitudes, values and beliefs, sensitivity to others' needs and opinions.

OFSTED (1994) recognises the contribution of dance to *pupils' spiritual, moral, social and cultural development*, which may be fostered through exploring a range of dance styles and traditions. For example, children's awareness and respect for different cultures, their aesthetic sensitivity, cooperation with peers in group work, and awareness of appropriate physical contact. It has to be said, with regard to the latter, that child-protection issues have tended to undermine the confidence of many teachers in engaging in movement and dance activities with their pupils. Schools vary in how they interpret the implications of recent directives in this area. Suffice it to say that dance work is contact-based: if children are at a stage in their social development where they are unable to organise their energy effectively in relation to their peers, then they will need to learn this in relation to an adult. The development of those children in movement and dance will be impoverished if staff are constrained by a 'hands-off' policy for staff, however well-intentioned.

Dance offers many opportunities to explore natural *curriculum links with the other arts* (and possibly economy in curriculum planning and timetabling!). The National Curriculum (DFE, 1995) specifically mentions children exploring moods and feelings in relation to music and rhythms through dance. Dance may reinforce appreciation in music, just as music may enhance quality and meaning in dance. Dance is also frequently associated with drama ('dance-drama'), particularly in conveying narrative through symbolic use of movement. There is a clear distinction however: dance is more abstracted in selecting significant moments, whereas in drama the narrative is conveyed 'as if' it were happening, even when it is mime. Both dance and art explore line, form and shape; dance may be used to intepret works of art: maybe bringing to life paintings or sculptures, or extending the portrayal of gesture or a static image (for example, the Northern Ballet Theatre's highly acclaimed production 'A Simple Man', based on the works of the artist L S Lowry). The DES (1992, para 2.1, p G7) identified the following links for dance across all the arts:

- the use of explicit aesthetic criteria to judge performance;
- concern with elements such as dynamics, pace, structure and stillness;
- concern with shape, line and form;
- the application of the skills of investigating, improvising, composing and appreciating.

Dance also has potential points of *contact with other subject areas* in the curriculum, and offers children the potential for more coherent, meaningful learning. Dance will have links not just with art but also with mathematics, in developing children's understanding of shape and three-dimensional form and structure. Dance may help consolidate number concepts, in the sequential counting of steps in certain routines. Dance will also contribute to children's understanding of forces in science, as they experience momentum and learn to organise their energy in relation to others (e.g. pushing, pulling, lifting, lowering, supporting, etc). Links may be made with geography, developing concepts of 'travelling' and following pathways and directions. Dance may lend significance to moments in history, to convey a narrative, or feelings or emotions of people under tension. Attention to the significance of body language, including gesture and facial expression, and subtleties of communication, contribute to the development of children's speaking and listening skills, including signing (English). While a non-verbal art, dance 'in process' may require considerable negotiation skills, as well as developing understanding of specific vocabulary through active learning par excellence!

Generally, movement will help foster the *development of children's study skills*. Their powers of observation and expression will develop as they learn to watch and listen. Their resourcefulness and sense of self-reliance will be fostered through encouraging their inventiveness in tasks that prompt divergent thinking and 'problem solving'. Focusing and directing themselves in physical tasks may help channel restless energy, and help develop children's concentration. Greater physical control and feeling 'at ease' in one's body may enable children to experience greater emotional control; movement and dance may provide an appropriate outlet for aggression or exertion of physical force. Movement and dance may provide an alternative means of expression in non-verbal form – thus elevating the status of alternative systems of communication, such as gesture and signing. Certain children with SEN may find themselves participating at the same level as their mainstream peers, and may be able to participate in integration programmes through dance, with the associated boost to their confidence and self-esteem.

Movement and dance will help develop the 'social health' of the group and an appropriate *atmosphere conducive to learning*, where individual achievements are valued and everyone is able to experience the satisfaction from success, and the associated boost to one's self-esteem. All movement and dance work should be conducted in a positive, enabling atmosphere based on negotiation, trust and cooperation, without the pressure of having to 'get it right'. Good dance practice exemplifies an interactive approach to teaching (Collis and Lacey, 1996), whereby children may be empowered to take increasing control and responsibility for their own learning through making choices and decisions that are perceived to have relevance and meaning. Integral to dance and movement work is the fostering of communication and the development of children's sociability. Chapter 2 will consider a framework for dance, to support teachers in meeting individual needs within the context of the group.

CHAPTER 2

A Framework for Dance

So how can one develop the ability to move creatively and expressively? This chapter will explore the foundations for developing educational dance work, based on Laban's (1948) principles of movement observation and analysis. In particular, it will focus on the *elements of dance*, and indicate their significance for developing dance in schools. The chapter will begin by exploring the notion of one's own 'natural dance' as a starting-point, and implications for planning movement and dance work to meet individual needs and for developing quality in movement. Consideration will also be given to certain neurophysical factors affecting motor development; these may be 'remediated' at the same time: the 'learning how to do dance while doing it' approach.

Developing quality in movement

'Natural dancers'

Imagine you are walking around in the space (the room) assigned for dance, perhaps a large classroom, gym, school hall, dance or drama studio. Try to get in touch with your natural, preferred gait:

- Are you a dawdler or do you tend to move briskly?
- Do you tend to meander or do you move purposefully with a clear 'end point'?
- Are you energetic and forceful in your movement or are you someone perhaps with 'light touch' and a tendency to be more delicate?
- Do you tend to be rather tense and contained or are you more relaxed and abandoned in your movement?

The premise is that everyone has their own 'natural dance'. This may sound rather precious but it does make sense! According to how you answered the

questions above, it may be that you have begun to identify your own potential starting-point for dance, with reference to certain *dynamics* in movement. What you have begun to consider, are:
- the length of *time* taken to move (slow or sustained?);
- the kind of pathway in *space* adopted (flexible or direct?);
- the *weight* involved (firm or fine?);
- the *flow* of energy preferred (bound or free?).

It is control over the range of these dynamics – and being able to harness them in combination – that ultimately enables the dancer to move expressively. In order to achieve maximum expressive potential, then, the dancer will need to work from his or her own natural starting-point and gradually 'discover' and develop control over other possibilities. This has implications for dance teaching, the premise being that by observing how children move it is possible to work towards 'correcting' lop-sided development. In any teaching group it is likely that to varying degrees a range of needs will be apparent. This has consequences for the teacher in planning for breadth and balance in dance work. Consider for a moment some of the children with whom you work. It is likely you could readily instance certain members of the group who:
- tackle everything at a terrific rate...and who perhaps need to learn to slow down?
- take forever at a task...and who need to learn to speed up?
- wander rather aimlessly...and need to acquire and retain a clear goal?
- are very rigid about their tasks...and who need to approach things more flexibly?
- are very 'ham-fisted' about their actions...and who need to develop greater sensitivity?
- are very 'light touch' about their actions...and who need to learn to harness their strength?
- are very tense and 'up-tight'...and who need to learn to relax more and 'let go'?
- are very 'loose'...and need to learn to 'contain' and channel their energy?

Of course these represent extreme examples. Many children with SEN characteristically may display such polarised movement – and so indeed may many of the mainstream population. For example, many children with Down's Syndrome tend to have weak muscle tone and may need to learn to amass greater strength in their movement. Many children with cerebral palsy experiencing spasticity of their limbs will be very 'bound' and may be encouraged to learn to 'let go' and relax body tension through experiencing free-flowing movement. Children with autism, apt to be lost in their own world, may need to learn to focus their movement more directly, especially in relation to other people. Children who are hyperactive, or have attention-deficit disorder, may benefit from learning to organise themselves to move more slowly in sustained actions.

The old adage is that 'you can tell a lot about someone from the way they move'. The implication is that bodily movement reveals something about one's inner self and that greater physical control may have additional benefits emotionally and psychologically (being able to channel restless energy, and improvement in concentration, for example). The gait of many people with learning difficulties belies a general lack of 'integration' – relative inability to make links; their movement is similarly 'disconnected' (Sherborne, 1990). Developing greater body awareness and a range of possibilities may contribute not only to improvement in gait, but also to the development of self-confidence and self-esteem, through feeling 'at home' in one's body. Learning to organise one's energy through adjusting one's strength in relation to other people will also help develop trust, co-operation and communication skills, and a sense of social 'well-being' (this will be explored in greater depth in chapter 3).

Movement dynamics

Let us return to our foray into the dance space! Imagine now that the floor has become very slippery and that you are following through with your whole body, and the effect this has on how you are moving. Try to analyse now how you have changed your 'walk' into a 'slide'. Have you altered:

- the length of time involved (is it slow or sustained)?
- the pathway through space (is it direct or flexible)?
- the weight of the action (is it firm or fine)?
- the kind of flow of energy involved (is it bound or free)?

Imagine, now, that the floor has now become very hot or perhaps sticky. Again, how do you need to alter the *dynamics* – the way you are moving – to accommodate the changes? What if you are now feeling pretty angry about all this and take out your exasperation by stamping about the room – until your boss suddenly enters, whereupon you recoil and begin to move rather timidly instead? It will be apparent that any action may be analysed according to the kind of dynamics involved. While we do not have to get 'bogged down' in trying to work out precisely which dynamics are involved in combination in any one particular movement, it is important to be aware that there may be a continuum of development along each axis. In other words, any movement will involve degrees of being:

- firm – fine
- direct – flexible
- sudden – sustained
- bound – free

These principles form the basis of Laban's (1948) influential movement analysis. He identified eight contrasting 'effort actions', which he considered exemplified how these dynamics are harnessed in combination, and which represent extreme ends of their respective continuum. This is illustrated in table form in figure 2.1.

Basic action	Weight	Space	Time	Flow
THRUST	firm	direct	sudden	bound
PRESS	firm	direct	sustained	free
WRING	firm	flexible	sustained	bound
SPLASH	firm	flexible	sudden	free
FLICK	fine	flexible	sudden	bound
DAB	fine	direct	sudden	bound
GLIDE	fine	direct	sustained	free
FLOAT	fine	flexible	sustained	free

Figure 2.1: Laban's 'effort actions'

Figure 2.2 shows how these effort actions may be considered in relation to one another. Note how, in their respective pairings, one dynamic changes in order to affect the quality and meaning to create the action at the other end of the notional continuum. Skilled dancers will be able to integrate dynamics in combination, in order to lend meaning and significance to a movement, to make dance interesting; they will also be able to make fluent transitions from one kind of movement to another.

Some people will feel more comfortable than others in moving in certain ways according to their 'natural dance'. This may not be so very extreme but nonetheless the implication is that we could all be plotted somewhere along the various axes. Our obligation as teachers of dance is two-fold. Firstly, to enable our students to feel confident, initially, through consolidating their awareness and understanding of their natural movement starting-point. Secondly, to extend their expressive repertoire by introducing challenges of 'discovering' other movement possibilities, along the respective axes.

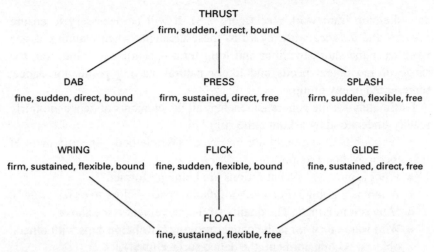

Figure 2.2: The relationship of Laban's 'effort actions' to one another

The elements of dance

The movement *dynamics* described above, when harnessed within dance, may lend significance and meaning, and give interest. Laban (1948) also identified other elements for dance, all of which may be used in combination with one another (see figure 2.3). In music and art the elements exist in a mutually supportive way, although in any one piece one element may have more significance than others: colour in painting, texture in orchestral pieces that feature contrasts with solo playing, etc. So it is the same with the elements of dance: for example, when Nureyev lifted Fonteyn above head height he was making a dramatic statement about the *relationship* of the two dancers, and lending significance also to the movement through use of *space*, and *body shape*. Laban's analysis of movement was summarised thus by Lowden (1989):

> ...dance is ACTION performed by the BODY in SPACE and TIME; significance is given by the spatial and temporal organisation, by the DYNAMIC qualities and the RELATIONSHIPS that occur (p. 44)

Planning dance work in schools needs to be driven by offering pupils in-depth experience of the elements of dance. It is preferable to plan a lesson that will address *one* of the elements in particular in order to focus pupils' awareness, and to expand their repertoire of movement possibilities related to that element (for example, exploring the *action* of 'rolling', or 'open' and 'closed' body *shapes*, etc). This will be given detailed consideration in chapter 5. For the moment, however, the elements of dance are summarised as a skeleton framework (see figure 2.3). It will be necessary to ensure *breadth* and *balance* with regard to these elements when planning dance work over the short, medium and long term – bearing in mind, too, the range of movement needs and likely natural starting points for dance, represented in any group.

Fortunately for the generalist teacher, all the elements of dance are fairly readily understood by asking quite simply:

- *Which* bits of the body are involved? (Whole body, specific parts of the body, body shape?)
- *What* is moving? (What actions are being performed?)
- *Where* is it going? (Personal or general space – close to or far away?)
- *How* is it moving? (The quality of the movement – see above)
- *With whom or what* is the dancer moving? (Relationships with others, objects, accompaniment, the dance surface itself).

How the body is moving – dynamics influencing the quality of movement – has already received some consideration in the previous section. The other elements will now be explained briefly.

The body

Which parts the dancer is moving – the body as a whole entity, or else certain parts – may be emphasised within a dance; for example, an elbow leading a spin. The *body's shape* or design will also give expressive potency to a movement. For example: angular, extended, round, twisted, etc. Some youngsters naturally may have unusual but potentially very interesting body shapes, which may lend design to dance work. Supporting staff will have responsibility to ensure that they enhance the child's shape – moving in an integrated way 'as one', rather than seeing themselves as an 'add on'.

Feeling the *whole body* moving through space is an important, integrating experience and will give awareness of the body's form. This flow of movement is equivalent to the sensation of driving over a bump in the road – that 'helter skelter' feeling that reminds you that you are all 'one'. This awareness may need to be 'fed in' to the developmentally young 'dancer' – being swung, slid, rocked, etc. (see chapter 3). Movement and dance work will need to be planned in accordance with a particular child's stage of neurophysical development – especially significant for those experiencing motor difficulties. Certain patterns of movement development will govern potential motoric possibilities; there is a specific developmental progression which affects emerging control of the head, trunk and limbs, and of the musculature (see section on Physical Considerations below).

BODY Which parts?	Whole Part Shape Action	symmetrical, asymmetrical isolated, emphasised round, broad, thin, twisted bend stretch twist	
ACTION What?	Activity	travel (including transfer of weight) balance (stopping, holding stillness) jump turn gesture	
SPACE Where?	Personal General Size of movement Direction Level Pathway	close to and around the body all the space in the area small or large forwards, backwards, sideways, around high, low, medium on the floor, in the air	
DYNAMICS How?	Time Tension Flow Space	sudden – sustained quick – slow firm – fine strong – light smooth – hesitant going – stopping direct – flexible linear – wavy	Combinations of: • 2 elements e.g. firm and sudden • 3 elements e.g. light, sustained and flexible • 4 elements e.g. light, sudden direct and bound
RELATIONSHIP With whom/what?	Proximity Sequence Spatial relationship Supporting Groupwork	near, far, approaching, retreating, surrounding canon, matching, opposing, question-answer, copying, mirroring, leading-following above, below, beside, around lifting, lowering, pushing, pulling, carrying numerical variation, group shape, inter-group relationship, alone in a mass	

Figure 2.3: The elements of dance

Focusing on specific *body parts* is also important in developing the dancer's knowledge of his/her body and its expressive potential. Selecting a particular body part as a theme for a movement and dance lesson may contribute to the children's overall body awareness by enabling them to feel that particular body part more keenly. (This will be considered in greater depth in chapter 4; refer also to examples of lessons in the Appendix, which highlight the development of particular parts of the body.) For example:

The centre (trunk) This is particularly important as the body's co-ordinating link, although the hardest body part for children to see (the last to emerge in their figure drawings). Awareness of the trunk will be reinforced through experiences of bending, stretching, twisting, pulling limbs into midline to curl up; also movement activities that involve tensing the trunk muscles, to exert effort. Contact of the trunk against the floor or against other people will also provide feedback of body image.

Knees and hips Awareness of the body's 'shock absorbers' is important for managing the weight and control over the lower part of the body.

Peripheries Awareness of the expressive potential of hands, feet and elbows.

Facial expression This helps give meaning and intention to a dance.

Actions

Essentially, there are four basic kinds of *actions*, in addition to holding stillness: travelling, jumping, turning, and gesturing. All action vocabulary will fall into these categories; for example:

travelling: run, walk, plod, crawl, drift, dash, dart, slither, slide, whiz, creep, shuffle, rush, stride, prowl, skim, drag, zoom, tip-toe, whoosh, retreat, stamp, dodge, etc.

jumping: bounce, pounce, leap, explode, skip, hop, soar, fly, gallop, spring, pop, launch, bubble, plunge, etc

turning: roll, rotate, swirl, spin, coil, spiral, wind, whirl, whip, etc

gesture: twine, twist, pierce, tap, quiver, shrink, push, recoil, clap, point, tip, wrap, lean, expand, swell, extend, reach, pull, collapse, crumple, enclose, scatter, flop, shake, squeeze, gather, stretch, jerk, curl, contract, entangle, wring, smooth, grip, open, close, throw, duck, hit, etc.

stopping: hover, brake, freeze, complete, halt, hesitate, pause, settle, balance, hide, listen, look, etc.

Children may not be familiar with a particular action word but through movement their understanding will grow. Rosamund Shreeves (1979) notes the value of these action words as the basis for developing dance:

- they act as the *catalysts* for starting off movement invention, e.g. how many ways can you bounce?
- they may be used to give *practice* in movement, e.g. can you lift your knees as you run?
- they may be *linked* in sequences of action phrases, e.g. tip-toe–leap–flop
- they may be *combined* to make more complex actions, e.g. skipping with opening and closing arms.

Shreeves (1979) also indicates the importance of children experiencing *contrasts* in movement in order to highlight awareness of extreme movement possibilities:

- *'going and stopping' phrases*: in order to develop awareness of ebb and flow;
- *body part contrasts*: using one part of the body after another, or performing contrasting actions with the same body part;
- *contrasts in quality*: varying tension, speed, pathway, and strength of movements in juxtaposition.

Children need to develop their control, co-ordination, balance, poise and elevation in the basic actions of travelling, jumping, turning, gesture and stillness. Also, increasingly, they need to develop fluency and flexibility in moving in different ways: learning to transfer weight onto different body parts, developing awareness of posture, and refining transitions between movements to give continuity; and, additionally, increasing the complexity and subtlety of body actions, and learning to enrich them, through varying shape, dynamics and use of space combined in different ways.

Use of space

Where the dancer moves may be considered in relation to:

- *levels*: high (standing, flight – above the ground), low (on or along the ground) or mid-level (stooping or kneeling)
- *directions*: forwards, backwards, sideways, around
- *pathways*: along the floor or traced in the air (e.g. circular, zig-zags, grid, figure-of-eight, spiral, wavy etc).

All children including those with mobility difficulties will need to experience a full range of possibilities regarding use of space. The responsibility, then, is on able-bodied participants to ensure that the child using a wheelchair is able to experience movement above the ground, by being lifted through space and also along the ground, possibly on a blanket. Wheelchair-users may only be able to move independently in straight lines; they will need support to enable them to experience flexible, meandering pathways.

Children may need to be encouraged to explore directionality: they may opt to travel around the dance space in a particular direction (often anti-clockwise!), and may need to be urged to find different pathways. Some children may be confident (even over confident) in using all the 'general space' available; others may be more diffident and naturally prefer to work close to the body, in 'personal space' – they may be reluctant to share this with others. Whatever, children need to be encouraged gradually to 'push their boundaries', and to be challenged to use space in a range of ways, using large or small movements.

Relationships

The *proximity* with which the dancer moves and orientates in relation to other people, with or without contact, may give meaning; for example, moving towards, away from or around another person; also, relative *positioning* – above, below, behind, in front of or beside. The *sequence* of actions may be significant: matching in unison, often to spectacular effect on a large scale (corps de ballet, chorus lines, etc.); in canon (one after another), or else opposing (different actions performed by different dancers), copying, mirroring or leading-and-following.

Exerting force against one another will enable dancers to contain, support, lift, lower, push, pull or carry one another – all of which may contribute meaning, according to whether this is 'in harmony' or 'in opposition'. Such movement experiences in their own right, however, will be important for children learning to manage their strength and organise their energy (the 'people as apparatus' principle – Sherborne, 1990). Veronica Sherborne set particular store on **relationship play** as the means by which children will also learn to develop quality of movement (see chapters 3 and 4). Involving children early in these kinds of experience will incidentally foster the social health of the group and enable children to work together in groups; ultimately, this will facilitate them co-operating to devise and choreograph their own pieces.

Physical considerations

In developing movement and dance work, recognition needs to be given to children's physical development, since their expressive potential will necessarily be affected by their co-ordination and any limiting factors, as in the case of those with children experiencing physical disability. This need not restrict their active participation, however – far from it, since specific movement experiences may be targeted to meet an individual need. For the teacher working with a group with wide-ranging abilities, the challenge will be to *differentiate* teaching, to meet all the needs some of the time, meanwhile engaging the whole group in purposeful activity. (Developing quality in dance teaching will be considered in greater depth in chapter 7.) Teachers may need to be imaginative in how they ensure the curricula entitlement of all their pupils (see chapter 1) and in how they access different movement experiences for certain children; for example:

- enlarging limited movement by attaching lengths of ribbon (to the finger, foot, etc.)

- exploring changes of level afforded by children seated in wheelchairs
- emphasising interesting body shapes, by having supporting staff mirror or expand these shapes with their own body
- moving children on blankets or sturdy lengths of fabric, to explore flexibility and travelling on different levels
- connecting children with sturdy lengths of elastic, to enable them to experience tension against one another.

The teacher will need to be aware of certain governing principles concerning processes of physical development, in planning movement and dance work to meet a range of needs.

1. Patterns of development

Movement and physical development of the young child follows two parallel sets of patterns:

(a) *Cranial development apparently precedes cordal (cephalo-caudal development)* That is, the child is able to look towards a stimulus, then lift the head by pushing up from the shoulders (suggesting emergent control of the trunk), then control the trunk to sit, before gaining control over the lower body (hips, knees, ankles, and finally feet for walking);

(b) *The child develops centrally first, then laterally (proximo-distal development)* That is, the child develops control from the centre of the body outwards to the extremities (i.e. use of the shoulder, action from the elbow and then wrist before the hands).

Children need to become articulate movers of the upper and lower body. They should experience these fundamental movement patterns and work towards improving the quality of the basic actions (travelling, jumping, turning) and a range of locomotion skills. Veronica Sherborne (1990) set particular store by an 'earthing' principle for developing movement work with children. She advocated that, initially, children should develop their confidence and motor abilities on the floor and gradually work up to kneeling and standing (balancing on an increasingly narrow base); ultimately children may confidently leave the surface ('flight') and land safely, managing their weight in relation to the floor from different levels. Sherborne maintained this principle should run through every movement and dance session, as well as influencing longer-term planning. It will affect how programmes of work in dance are designed, as children may need to recapture the cephalo-caudal sequence of development:

- developing awareness of the centre as the co-ordinating link and learning to manage the trunk by rolling over
- moving along the floor with the trunk in contact, using the shoulders for propulsion
- moving from sitting, involving transfer of weight onto the hands to give momentum
- transferring weight to move on hands and knees
- moving on hands and feet
- developing locomotion skills from standing
- transferring body weight to a single foot, to hop along and to take off (jump)
- acquiring strength in the pelvis for it to remain horizontal, in order to develop balances (holding stillness) and hopping on the spot.

Furthermore, because control over limbs develops 'down the arm', this implies that a child with energetic gross-motor actions (from the shoulder) will need to consolidate these actions in movement work: until control is gained over such energy, the child will not be capable of delicacy and 'fine touch' in fine-motor actions. It stands to reason that subtlety in using gesture may be beyond the potential of such a pupil otherwise. Children may need a considerable length of time to achieve competence in those parts of the limbs that are relatively distant from the centre of the body. Supporting staff will have a crucially important role: gradually fading out the amount of assistance so that children increasingly take more and more of their own weight through their limbs.

It follows that brain damage or damage to the central nervous system will impair motor functioning, or cause delayed motor development. In movement education, the aim is to feed in 'normal' input to achieve 'normal' output; for example, reducing the effects of spasticity by attempting to reverse patterns: loosening the shoulder by pushing down and encouraging the child to take his/her own weight on arms; learning to transfer weight in movement activities that involve the child rocking from side to side in a sitting position. Another implication is that however physically limited a dancer, communication may be achieved through focusing on areas of strength; for example, a small gesture, or the power of holding stillness, or the expressive potential of the head and face.

2. Types of movement

There are three basic types of movement; these too follow a developmental pattern:

(a) *Flexion* (e.g. bending) The flexor muscles are the first set to develop (for 'pulling in' movements), facilitating internal rotation and adduction (pulling in to the mid-line);

(b) *Extension* (e.g. stretching) The extensor muscles (from the back) develop next, enabling external rotation and abduction (movement away from mid-line);

(c) *Rotation* (e.g. twisting) The ability to turn needs to emerge before a joint can be locked into extension; this is the last type of movement to emerge, but also the first to go when development is interrupted, resulting characteristically in lack of flow or flexibility.

A child will need experiences of all three types of movement: flexion, extension and rotation. Warm-up activities for movement and dance should ensure children are offered opportunities to limber up these three sets of muscular actions in exercises involving bending, stretching and twisting. A child who is developmentally restricted in movement, or else perhaps exaggerated in moving in a particular mode (e.g. excessive ataxic actions), will need particular consideration given to his or her physical starting-point and potential movement possibilities. The developmental sequence is significant when encouraging a new skill; for example, a child will be able to lift the leg before taking weight through it. When damage is experienced frequently there is regression to the first set of movement patterns (flexion), to a typical 'collapsed' posture; the child may need to begin working again from the new movement starting-point and learn to rediscover other types of movement, as far as possible.

3. Musculatory development

Movement at any joint goes through four developmental stages:

(a) *Light work – unskilled* For example a baby flailing arms and legs, reflex actions, rolling of the head, twiddling, etc. Frequently movements are comforting, although there may be social pressures to inhibit them (e.g. finger play), which may be culturally relative (compare north and south European attitudes to use of hands in expression).

(b) *Heavy work – holding* For example, the child starts to raise the head slightly. Tension begins in the musculature; this needs to develop in every joint before it can be relaxed.

(c) *Heavy work – movement* For example, the child, having lifted the head and taken weight on the shoulders, begins to move forward and transfers weight on to all fours.

(d) *Light work – skilled* More sophisticated movements develop, for example, the use of tongue and lips, face muscles, hand manipulation and walking.

It will be apparent that the child gradually develops more discriminating movement responses. There is a notion of 'movement readiness', when a child may have acquired sufficiently mature structure and musculature to attempt a more advanced procedure. For example, lack of tone in the muscles (typical in Down's Syndrome) will mean that the stimulus for the musculature to respond appropriately is not received effectively; lack of tension will prevent bones from developing solidly – hip sockets are frequently loose in children with Down's Syndrome, hence the need to compensate with movement to develop extensor muscle tone. It follows, also, that until children can support their weight on to the arms and transfer weight they will be unable to pick up, hold or replace objects. The shoulder muscles can be *trained* through movement experiences that require the children to take their weight and to use force.

An implication for dance work is that all children will need plenty of movement experiences that involve tensing and exerting force. They will then become capable of 'letting go' of their energy in more relaxed, lightweight and delicate or flowing movement, and of developing control over subtle use of gesture and grip. Laban (1948) recognised that the actual impulse given to nerves and muscles which move the joints of our limbs originates in *inner efforts*. Kephart (1960) pointed out that the central nervous system is organised not in terms of anatomical segments but in *movement patterns*: it is through experience and experimentation that the child learns to innovate the muscle groups involved. To achieve quality in movement, the children will need to pass through the sequence of cephalo-caudal development (see above), and be able to harness the musculature to control their energy and the amount of strength required.

This chapter has indicated the value and importance to the developing child (and emerging dancer!) of sensori-motor experiences. This principle is embodied in Veronica Sherborne's (1990) creative movement programme, which will be considered now in depth. Chapter 3 will describe how children may learn to organise their strength in relation to other people. Chapter 4 will develop this further, and explore ways to recapture stages of physical development indicated above. Essentially, the movement experiences Sherborne promoted may provide the potential content for planning developmentally appropriate dance work across the age and ability range.

CHAPTER 3

Developing Control of Energy

Control over energy is crucial for anyone wishing to move creatively and expressively. Veronica Sherborne (1990) advocated that this was best effected through a 'people as apparatus' principle: learning to adjust and control one's strength in relation to other people through *relationship play*. This aspect of movement work, based on recapturing principles of early sensori-motor experiences, will be considered in this chapter. Additionally, one will need to acquire knowledge of the *body* – which *parts* are moving (whole body or particular parts), the kind of *shapes*, and basic *actions* (travelling, jumping, turning, gesture and holding stillness). This second major strand to creative movement will be explored more fully in chapter 4.

Getting in touch

Through 'rough and tumble' toddler-type play, young children develop their awareness of others: *directly*, through channelling energy in relation to another person; they may also receive feedback *indirectly* of their body image, through contact of the body against other people in different movement experiences. The importance of these early sensori-motor experiences to child development was discussed in chapter 1. Sherborne (1990) formalised examples of 'rough and tumble' movement experiences into a developmental sequence, to provide a framework for developing quality in movement (see figure 3.1). Essentially, this creative movement programme indicates the inter-relationship of the elements of dance (see figure 2.3). By harnessing movement experiences appropriately, therefore, it is possible to foster children's emerging expressive potential of their bodies. This may be achieved through requiring children to exert effort to different degrees, and by reinforcing their awareness of their body in action.

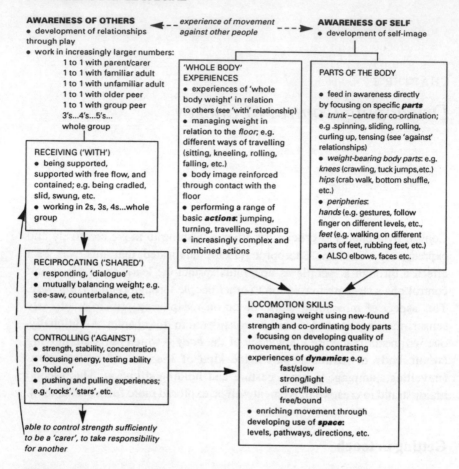

Figure 3.1: A developmental creative movement programme (after Veronica Sherborne, 1990)

Many young children will arrive in school with rudimentary ability – or with the potential – to move confidently and imaginatively. Indeed, the implication is that it is the job of the nursery teacher to help give this ability greater form, so that by the time they enter formal schooling children are able to move with increasing control and co-ordination and an awareness of space and others (SCAA, 1996a). It is assumed, perhaps, that many children will have benefited from the kind of early physical play with carers described above. However, some children with learning difficulties may not experience (or have experienced) this kind of relationship play as an infant. This may be for several reasons:

- the reaction perhaps of shocked parents to a disabled child may result in the infant not receiving the usual kind of physical handling;

- the relative inability of a child to partake in early reciprocal interactions with parent/carer (either because of limited responses or because of a physical disability) may be a disincentive, and result in lack of attention and therefore stimulation;
- hypotonic condition may influence the quantity and quality of handling the disabled child receives, so that s/he may receive less stimulation than normal;
- parental expectations may be lower from their disabled child, therefore relatively little is expected in the way of movement and other development;
- a disabled child may be 'over-protected' and thus sheltered from the stimulation of being handled by others and experiencing sensory stimulation generally.

Whether or not this happens to be the case in a particular instance, it *is* the case that *all* may benefit from 'recapturing' (and revisiting) the kind of progression in interactive relationship play, commonly seen in early childhood (see figure 3.1), as a basis for developing communication, both verbal and non-verbal. This may be on a conscious level: eye contact, vocalising, and negotiating with others in movement experiences and to create dances – discovering too, of course, the power of dance as a means of communication 'without words'. Communication may also develop on an unconscious level through improvement in the quality of interpersonal relationships, which will ultimately benefit children being able to work co-operatively. For many children with learning difficulties, movement work may be an important opportunity to foster their personal and social development. However, the social health of *any* group may be improved across the age and ability range through judicious partnering of participants.

Many movement experiences will require children to trust their weight to another person. In this way, they may acquire the physical confidence to 'let go' – to be supported, contained or handled by another – and also emotional confidence and security. Their self-confidence may be enhanced by investing them with a sense of responsibility: taking the role as the 'carer' in partner or group work, to 'look after' another. The quality of the contact offered by the carer is crucial: much is transmitted through the sense of touch. This requires a degree of social maturity and responsibility; however, it is also possible for this to be *fostered* through the movement experiences themselves – again, 'learning how to do it whilst doing it'! Occasionally it may be appropriate to take some calculated risks: children can often show surprising sensitivity and consideration towards those that are younger or more vulnerable.

It is possible to follow a developmental progression in organising partners:
- parent – child
- regular staff – child
- unfamiliar adult – child
- older peer – child
- same age friend – child
- same age peer – child
- younger child – child

Gradually, group work may be introduced, again along a developmental progression. Initially perhaps this would be in natural friendship groups, in which the child is more likely to feel relaxed and confident, trusting enough to tackle new challenges; then in mixed groupings with peers that are not necessarily first-choice friends! The teacher can certainly be strategic in manipulating social dynamics; for example, placing a supporting adult to work within a certain grouping. Children may work together in groups of three, four or five, or even the whole class together. Developmentally young children may not have sufficient maturity to work co-operatively with one another. Nevertheless, they may begin to work towards this in groups with socially more mature peers or in movement experiences where they are required to carry out an action on an adult: their attention will often be so riveted on the adult involved that children may find themselves co-operating quite unconsciously alongside one another in this way. Similarly, they may be required to 'do their bit' to maintain a body shape or structure; for example, alongside one another on hands and knees, to create a human tunnel or bridge.

'Role reversal' experiences, whereby the young child 'looks after' an adult or older child, can be very valuable in terms of social relations: implicit is the statement by the older person to the child 'I trust you', which is empowering to the child, as well as confidence raising. This may all seem very staff-intensive. However, it may be possible to work creatively on this, and in fact to foster very purposeful links within the school and/or with the wider community. For example:
- parents coming into school to work with their own child in a movement session
- younger and older children linking up within the school
- maximising available students on placement within the school
- offering work experience placements to young people
- developing links between classes in a mainstream and special school.

The emphasis needs to be on fun and enjoyment: an informal, non-competitive atmosphere where everyone may succeed. There should be a spirit of shared adventure, where everyone's achievements are valued and all may experience a sense of self-worth. The teacher needs to be prepared to tolerate higher noise thresholds than usual: movement experiences frequently prompt spontaneous laughter, giggling and vocalisation. The teacher may well wish to exploit opportunities to develop children's communication skills, such as understanding of specific vocabulary (especially verbs – action words; and prepositional understanding – over, under, through, etc); also opportunities for children to engage in dialogue to negotiate 'solutions' in partner and group work. In a sense there is a shift in status between teacher and pupils: teacher provides the germ of an idea, but does not have the 'right answer'. This in itself may prompt pupils to relate to the teacher more informally, and to use a different kind of language. (It may be necessary to set clear boundaries for certain pupils on what is or is not acceptable or appropriate, to avoid this being abused.)

Relationship play

The aim of relationship play (and indeed of educational dance) is to enable participants to get in touch with bodily experience, not through mechanical exercise but rather from the inner sensation resulting from movement itself. In time, this awareness may be shaped to enable the person to use body language communicatively and expressively. How a person moves can be indicative of his or her inner state (as suggested in chapter 2), and how he or she relates to the outer world and to other people. It is not the case that one has to wait until a moment when a child is magically 'ready for dance'. It is important even in early movement work to infuse awareness of *quality of movement*, through contrasting experiences in juxtaposition. In this way, even very young children will begin to discover a range of movement possibilities with the elements of *dynamics* and *use of space*. For example: a slow sustained activity followed by a fast or sudden one, moving in straight lines then wiggly pathways, tensing then relaxing, moving forcefully then lightly, moving up high then down low, moving expansively around the room then in localised space, etc.

Relationship play is based on the same developmental pattern as early childhood 'rough and tumble' play. Initially the infant is on the *receiving* end of movement experiences: being contained and supported by the carer, often with flowing movements built in; for example, being cradled, swung, rocked, etc. The emphasis is on feeding in a sense of value and self-esteem and working for reactions, and for these to become more consistent responses – eye-contact, vocalisation and smiles. The infant then begins to engage in movement experiences requiring mutual, reciprocal *sharing* of energy – the classic see-saw or counter-balance principle. The infant may begin to initiate and introduce new ideas into the situation. Finally, then, the child becomes *controlling* and intentionally exerts force against the carer, perhaps in mock 'battles' involving pushing over and pulling along. It is only when a child has learned control over energy in this way that he or she will be able to adjust energy levels sensitively and responsibly, to 'look after' another with sufficient delicacy and *'fine touch'*.

Movement experiences are not 'once and forever': they constantly need revisiting and repeating, even if couched in different contexts – 'the lesson for the teacher and the lesson for the pupils'. Figure 3. 2 illustrates this as a spiral: points of intersection with the dotted line indicate benchmarks in progress towards developing sensitivity and 'fine touch'. The coils of the spiral, however, are the movement experiences; these enlarge as the child's movement repertoire expands but represent a circuitous, variable route towards achieving progress. Planning movement experiences should begin from a child's present level of ability. Some new movement experiences may be introduced in a more directed way (teacher demonstrating or initiating), which the children may then try out for themselves, take on and elaborate. Children will also need to repeat and consolidate their skills and confidence in familiar movement experiences. Equally, they will also need to be encouraged to be inventive and 'explore': children may be very original in their movement ideas, and may learn from one another in this way. The teacher may then build and extend (akin to Bruner's [1986] 'scaffolding' model), in order to lead the child(ren) to new levels of achievement.

The teacher will have a notion of where it is all heading but may confidently take cues from the children, so reinforcing their actions and giving a sense of intention and significance to their movement. Plainly, the way movement experiences are presented will be crucial: it is simply undignified for adolescents to be engaged in see-saws and encouraged to hum along to the nursery rhyme 'See-saw Marjory-daw'. However, the same experience may be more appropriately introduced as a challenge for such pupils: for example 'sit on the floor facing your partner... now grip your partner's wrists just enough so that they feel secure you won't let go.... now see if you can both rock forwards and backwards in slow motion...' The same pupils may even acquire more readily this ability to give and take of their energy if partnering a much younger or more vulnerable child. As intimated above, taking such calculated risks can often pay off, not just in fostering the child's developing physical maturity: implicit is the investment of responsibility and trust in the child and a boost to his or her self-esteem.

Adult

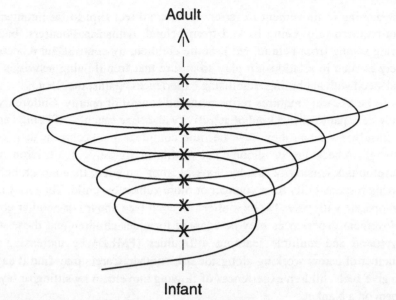

Infant

Figure 3.2: Developing dance: a spiral curriculum

Receiving relationships

Characteristically in these types of movement experiences, the 'carer' takes the weight of the recipient, to support or contain. Building in a sense of flowing movement will feed in an awareness of the body moving through space – the 'helter skelter' feeling when the car drives over a bump in the road. It is a case of recapturing the essence of the kind of interactive play that takes place with a young baby: gentle bouncing, rocking, cradling, working for eye contact, smiles, giggling, etc. The carer invests these pleasurable responses with meaning, and takes them as a sign that the baby wants the interaction to continue. Carers also tend to build in an ebb and flow quite intuitively with a young baby, punctutating activity with 'pregnant pauses' that foster a sense of anticipation, and introducing contrasts in movement: moving and stopping, rocking up high then down low, etc.

The carer will be looking for signals that the child is relaxed during movement experiences (e.g. dropping head right back, feet flopping outwards, etc.); it is a sign of self-confidence when the child can shut his or her eyes. Paradoxically, however, clinging can also be a positive indication of involvement in rough and tumble play, as the child is demonstrating a willingness to commit his or her weight and trust to the carer. Some people will have an ambivalence towards contact with others. They may find it less threatening in movement experiences where direct face to face contact is not required (e.g. being rocked from behind, lying across carers' backs, being swung from behind, etc.). Some children, by contrast, may become very excited in relationship play so ensure that free flowing activities are balanced with anchoring, stabilising experiences against the floor.

To be a 'carer' requires refinement and control of energy. Children will only be capable of this kind of sensitivity and 'fine touch' – of being carers themselves – when they have become confident and secure in their own strength (check the developmental profile in figure 3.1). Children may develop this sensitivity first by 'looking after' an adult, then a peer, before taking responsibility for a younger or more vulnerable child. They may also co-operate with peers to 'look after' an adult (see above) or another child. Movement experiences may be adapted for older children and those with profound and multiple learning difficulties (PMLD) by increasing the number of carers working alongside one another. Carers may find it easier to give such children experiences of flowing movement by sitting or laying them on a blanket.

In part, the following examples of 'relationship play' movement experiences are drawn from the useful Appendix in *Developmental Movement for Children* (Sherborne, 1990). Note that the term 'carer' does not necessarily imply an adult but rather the person with responsibility for taking charge of another (and who therefore may be another child); in certain activities, however, it will be apparent that an adult is required.

Supporting – commitment of weight

- Carer sitting or lying on the floor, face down or face up (see figure 3.3), child lies or sits astride the carer (less threatening when the carer is lower than the child), engage in nursery play: feed in awareness of the trunk in a lively, flexible way, through body contact, tickling, bouncing, patting, etc.

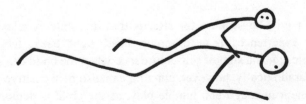

Figure 3.3: Low level 'ride'

- As above: carer gives the child a ride, keeping back or stomach flat on the floor; precede by gently bouncing, to get the child used to the movement
- Carer on all fours: child astride adult's back (see figure 3.4) face down; sitting astride adult's back (as on a horse); sitting on adult's back and lying back (adult to sway slightly)

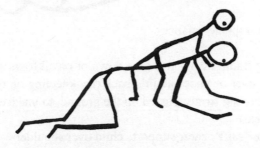

Figure 3.4: 'Ride' on all fours

- Carer on all fours (as above), gives child a ride, carrying round in different ways (as above)
- Carer on all fours, child lies face down across carer's back, pivoting centrally; carer gives child a ride (see figure 3.5)

Figure 3.5: 'Pivot' ride

- Carer sits on floor, knees bent and feet on ground, child sits on carer's knees or lies along them
- Carer sitting, child stands on bent knees
- Carer on all fours, child stands on back
- 'Aeroplane balance' (see figure 3.6): carer supine on floor, child prone on adult, carer bends knees and raises child to support mid-air, maintaining hand-grip

Figure 3.6: 'Aeroplane balance'

- 'Climbing frame': carer lies face down or on all fours – child slithers or climbs over or under adult's back (try kneeling on one knee, with foot of other leg firmly placed on the ground, to make a tree with lots of branches!)
- 'Firefighter's lift': carer supports child over shoulder
- Back to back: carer bends forward, and supports child on back (linked at elbows), lifting off the ground
- 'Somersault' (see figure 3.7): carer sits on floor, legs outstretched, with space for child to roll into, child somersaults over carer's shoulder (carer supports child, feeding in awareness of the trunk as the child curls over)

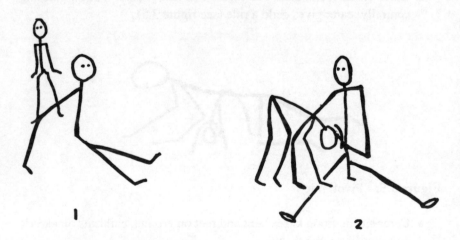

Figure 3.7: Forward somersault

- 'Rocking horse': three or four carers on all fours, lined up side by side, child to lie across carers' backs prone or supine (more threatening); carers may sway gently side to side, forwards and backwards or side to side; carers may move together to give the child a ride; to dismount, carers help the child to roll off by reaching behind with one arm to support the child, then kneeling up on heels so that the child rolls slowly to the ground with support

- Human 'physiotherapy ball': three or four carers make a star (bottoms together in the centre, carers facing outwards on all fours), child lies prone or supine across bottoms, and carers bounce gently

Containing – commitment by child to lean or cling

- Cradling (see figure 3.8): carer sits on floor behind child, and wraps round the child using the whole body, arms, trunk and thighs as support, carer rocks the child gently; child may take charge of carer, by standing or kneeling behind

Figure 3.8: 'Cradling'

- 'Houses': as above, but the carer uses arms and legs to make walls of a house (can be very comforting and secure!) or a 'prison' (the child has to try and escape – many often do not want to!)
- Carer kneels on all fours, enclosing the child (see figure 3.9), maybe walking or chasing round the room, to keep the child contained

Figure 3.9: Enclosed crawl

- Carer balances on hands and feet, hips in the air, child crawls underneath in different directions
- Enclosed spin: carer stands with firm base, knees slightly bent, arms open, child runs towards carer and leaps on the carer's waist, gripping with legs and arms (carer embraces child and may spin round with the momentum of the jump)
- 'Gibbons': carer on all fours, child clings on carer's underside, gripping round middle with legs, and arms round carer's neck (carer takes child for a ride)
- 'Tunnels': carer on all fours, child to crawl under in different ways (on back, on stomach, using hands/not using hands); several carers may make different tunnels; or perhaps a long line of carers on all fours – child to creep underneath (or along the top)

Supporting with free flow

- Carer cradles child from behind, sitting on floor (as above), tucking child up, carer tips child gently off balance; carer rocks child forwards and backwards, side to side; can become more energetic, tilting right back and sitting up; tilting right back may result in a backwards somersault, so that the child ends up standing behind the head of the carer lying on the floor (see figure 3.10)

1   2

Figure 3.10: Backward somersault

- Two carers sit facing each other, and rock child between them (see figure 3.11)

Figure 3.11 Rocking in threes

- 'Rocking horses' (see above)
- 'Aeroplanes' (see above)
- 'Trampette': carer sits, lies down or goes on all fours, child sits astride, carer bounces child gently
- Swinging: carer picks up child under the arms from behind, child faces away, carer swings child round; two carers (standing) make a swing seat for the child (cross hands or sailor's wrist grip); two carers (or more if child is large) each hold child's wrist and ankle and swing child through the air (see figure 3.12)

Figure 3.12: A shared 'swing'

- Jumping: carer extends forearms to child, child presses down on forearms or hands for support; two carers support the child under the arm and under the forearm, and shoot the child up into the air (see figure 3.13); carer makes a shape (elongated or curled up) on the floor for the child to step then jump over
- Vaulting: carer on all fours, takes weight of child on small of back and hips, child transfers weight onto hands on adult's back, and does a few small jumps (see figure 3.14); jumps may become higher and higher and springier; once hips are high, child may be encouraged to jump and twist over carer's legs

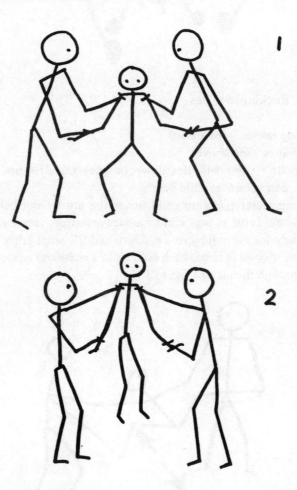

Figure 3.13: Supported jump

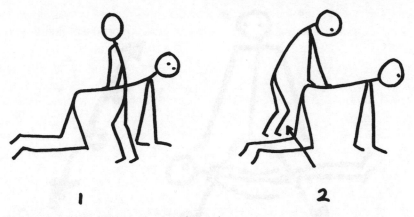

Figure 3.14: Vaulting – human horse!

- Sliding: child lies supine on floor, carer slides child by the ankles or wrists (see figure 3.15); child to be slid in straight or wavy lines, carer thus building in flexibility of the trunk
- Rolling: carer sits on floor with child lying across thighs, carer rolls child up and down the length of the thighs (see figure 3.16); carer lays child down on side (arm under head), and rolls child over by pushing or pulling (one hand on shoulder, one on the hip); double roll – carer and child roll as one (carer may contain child or both hold hands above the head)

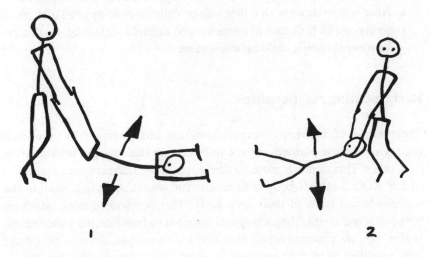

Figure 3.15: 'Sliding'

Figure 3.16: 'Rolling' across thighs

- 'Engine': carer and child sit back to back, child relaxes (head resting on carer's back, hands in lap, legs outstretched), and carer pushes child along using hands and feet for propulsion
- 'Problem package': child presents a problem (limp, rigid, tight ball, odd shape, etc.), two or more carers have to carry child to somewhere else in the room
- 'Logs': several carers lie next to one another, child lies across bodies, carers roll in unison, to move child along the human conveyor-belt
- Trust fall: two carers sit either side of child (tucked up) and rock child gently to and fro between them; maybe extend to standing, two carers (or more) pushing child between them

Reciprocating relationships

These kinds of movement experiences are characterised by a mutual sharing of energy: partners engage in balancing their weight in relation to each other. This is much more challenging, as the partners are required to 'listen' to each other's body with sensitivity, whilst being in control of the weight-bearing parts of their own body. This demands concentration on both parts, and channelling energy as opposed to free-flowing experiences. It also requires greater control over one's own weight, since to be a carer with a smaller, light child involves an adjustment to ensure that the child is given only as much weight to support as he or she can manage.

- See-saw: partners sit on the floor facing each other, holding by the wrists, each takes it in turn to lie backwards, head touching the floor, and to help partner to sit up (see figure 3.17); partners kneel on the floor and see-saw (as above); partners stand facing each other, arms extended, and support each other to see-saw up and down, forwards and backwards

Figure 3.17: See-saw from sitting position

- Sitting back to back: stand up and sit down, staying in contact (push hard, feet against the ground)
- Standing from sitting: partners sit facing each other, knees bent, feet apart in stable position, gripping each other securely by the wrists; both pull backwards and manage to stand up together; partners maintain mutual balance, to sit down again together
- Carer firmly based, knees slightly apart, child stands on carer's thighs (holding by wrists), carer and child both lean back
- Counter-balance: partners sit facing each other, holding by the forearms or wrists, both lean back (see figure 3.18); partners kneel facing each other, holding by forearms or wrists, both lean back; partners stand facing one another, holding by forearms or wrists, both lean back; partners support one another with one arm only (make shape with 'loose' arm), develop into a spin, varying heights

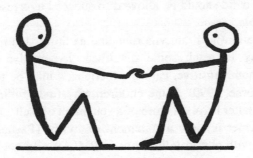

Figure 3.18: Counter-balance from sitting position

● Upside-down balance: partners lie on the floor with legs in the air, holding each other's wrists, pressing feet hard against partner's feet, so that they make an arch with their bodies, balancing on their shoulders

Controlling relationships

Controlling or 'against' relationships (Sherborne, 1990) entail children testing their strength against one another. They involve focusing of energy and attention, and may incidentally help promote the development of a child's ability to concentrate. While activities may appear 'mock battles', they are not really competitive as such, although the teacher may need to set them up carefully to avoid the context being abused. For example, it may be that prior to using partners as a vault, children are encouraged to test that their partner (on hands and knees) is really 'stuck tight' (a supporting 'with' relationship, but also a controlling 'against' one! – Sherborne, 1990). The intention is really to feed in a sense of firmness and stability in one's partner, by checking out his or her ability not to be shifted from their base. This will best be developed, initially, from experiencing steadiness close to the ground: the floor offers maximum support – a wide base; maintaining balance and stability on two feet is much more challenging.

It may be preferable for those new to movement work to experience 'shared' relationships initially, in order to appreciate an appropriate ethos. Then, perhaps, to begin to engage in these controlling or 'against' relationships with an adult before partnering a peer. The atmosphere needs to be fun and playful. Use a 'direct' approach: establish eye contact and confront the child from the front in a straight line, in order to feed in a sense of strength and determination. It is important not to destroy the feeling of stability by actually shifting the child off his/her base; however, the child should be 'tested' sufficiently (by being pushed or pulled) to use all his/her strength to maintain it. The carer needs to adapt the degree of resistance sensitively: the child should be allowed to succeed as a result of using all the effort possible.

'Against' relationships' are vigorous and exciting, and may provide an appropriate way to reach some disturbed, hyperactive or aggressive children for whom sensitive, caring experiences may be too threatening initially (Sherborne, 1990). Some children may find 'pulling' easier than 'pushing' – the latter involves more of a statement of 'self' against another, whereas the former is more a statement of 'wish' (Payne, 1992). Other children (those with physical disability or PMLD) may not be able to feel tension against one another so readily; using lengths and loops of sturdy elastic or plastic whirly tubes connected on elastic to connect them with a partner may enable them to gain something of the experience. It may not be appropriate for peers to pitch their strength against each other straightaway in this type of movement experience; this will be something to 'work towards', however. After all, dancers can be required to lift, lower, push, pull, support or carry one another – essentially these are 'against' relationships given meaningful significance (as with the earlier example of Nureyev lifting Fonteyn above head height).

Controlling activities 'against' a carer

- Child to help carer to stand up from the floor, by pulling up
- 'Engine' (see above): child to push carer along, sitting back to back on the floor
- Carer as 'parcel', child to undo carer, curled up into a ball
- 'Prison': carer sits behind child, carer's arms, body and thighs become walls of a prison, child tries to escape
- Child to roll carer over
- Carer lies on top of child, 'squashed' child to wriggle free
- Carer as 'rock' (see figure 3.19): carer sits with hands and feet securely flat on the ground, child 'tests' from front back and sides, before pushing carer over

Figure 3.19: 'Rocks'

- Carer as 'tent-pegged': carer kneels on one leg, the other bent out sideways holding the floor, to give a wide base, child pushes carer over

Controlling activities 'against' a peer

- 'Stars': one partner lies prone or supine and sticks hands and feet to the floor, the other tries to shift (see figure 3.20)

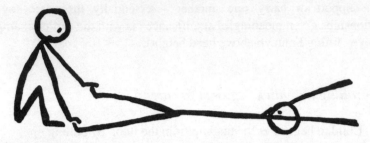

Figure 3.20: 'Stars'

- 'Tent-pegged' (see above)
- 'Rocks' (see above)
- Back to back: partners sit on floor back to back, each pushes against the other's back and attempts to shift partner along (see figure 3.21)

Figure 3.21: Pushing back to back from sitting position

- 'Prisoners': partners sit one behind the other (see 'prisons' above); two carers contain child with elbow and hand grip, 'prisoner' attempts to escape from standing position
- 'Parcels': one partner curls up tightly, the other tries to 'undo' (see figure 3.22)

Figure 3.22: 'Parcels' (maintaining closed body shape)

- 'Rocks' (see above)
- 'Sheriff': one partner stands, adopting wide base, knees bent, other tries to shift

Developing meaningful relationships

It is a small step to begin to infuse movement experiences with symbolic content (e.g. 'wriggling like wiggly worms' so prompting development of representational concepts and increasingly abstract thought). Use of stimuli (see chapter 6) may also help children to grasp that movement experiences may acquire metaphoric significance. Relationship play experiences themselves may also be extended and given dramatic meaning. For example, the teacher becomes a frightened monster which the children need to capture and look after. Wheeler (1995) provides another example: children sat one behind the other, one partner cradling the other; the person behind then became a strange creature holding tightly to its prey, so that a 'mock battle' ensued whereby the person had to 'escape' the creature. Relationship play experiences may be contextualised as part of an unfolding drama (see Peter, 1994) – another strategy in the drama teacher's carrier bag; for example, in a drama about pirates, movement work may provide moments of physical theatre:
- children may form a human tunnel (the smugglers' route to the ship)
- children may hold hands in a boat shape and sway in a group counter balance (simulating ship's movement)
- three children on hands and knees in a line may rock a fourth across their backs (to simulate the pirate sleeping in his cabin)

- a child may present a 'problem' for two pirates to deal with (a large stiff tree trunk to be transported for firewood, a round barrel of rum to be rolled along deck, etc.)
- two children may help a third to jump as high as possible (so that the pirate can reach and pick a luscious piece of fruit)
- half the class may make weird fantastical group shapes (dense undergrowth on the treasure island, through which the pirates have to crawl)

In relationship play, children may begin to grasp how to organise their bodies, and how to control their energy with the appropriate amount of effort. Physically exploring different ways of using energy in harmony and opposition will equip children with the knowledge of how this is achieved. This kind of insight may be contextualised subsequently in dance, to lend particular significance to an action. For example: dragging a slain soldier from the battle field, lifting a goal-scoring team member to carry him/her aloft, fantastical plants (weird group shapes) swaying in the breeze, etc. Pupils may be further extended by experiencing exertion of strength against a partner, then repeating this *without* physical contact, so that the opposition (or harmony) is *imagined*. For example: groups co-operating to lift a peer from lying down, to carry him/her keeping the body horizontal and still, and lowering the body carefully; then dancing in role as archaeologists, raising, carrying and lowering an imaginary Egyptian Mummy.

Through relationship play, an appropriate atmosphere will evolve for devising and participating in group dance, based on negotiation and co-operation. Children will learn to take turns and to consider and accept other people's ideas. In relationship play, children learn to trust, respect and understand the actions of others. Basic acceptance of turn-taking will make it possible for children to take part subsequently in dance where the spotlight may be on others within the group at certain moments, and where it may be important to maintain stillness in order not to 'up-stage' one another. Principles of working in harmony or opposition will spill over into consideration of performing actions in unison or in canon that match or contrast. Children may also become more aware of how the meaning of an action may be altered, according to how it is performed in relation to other members of the group: towards (approaching), away from (retreating), surrounding, near to or far away.

Through relationship play, participants of all ages and abilities will incidentally become more aware of their bodies as they make contact with others, and also with the floor. This emerging awareness of 'self' as opposed to others will be particularly significant for the developmentally young. This developing awareness of the body and its possiblities will also need to be consolidated in movement work that focuses explicitly on actions and parts of the body used in mobility. Chapter 4 will explore this aspect in detail.

CHAPTER 4

Developing Body Awareness

This chapter considers movement experiences to foster the development of children's awareness of their bodily potential for movement. As with the previous chapter, it is rooted in the developmental approach to movement promoted by Veronica Sherborne (1990). This offers a means also to remediate aspects of physical development (see chapter 2: children's respective stages of neurophysical development will be a necessary consideration in identifying starting-points for movement work). As indicated in previous chapters, however, it is a matter of 'learning how to do dance while doing it': harnessing appropriate movement experiences to meet particular needs, within the context of a dance lesson. This should be based on the respective National Curriculum key stage requirements for the child's chronological age. (Note that for health and safety reasons a physiotherapist should be consulted before embarking upon movement work with children with physical impairment.)

Awareness of the whole body

Experiences of free flowing movement, such as bouncing and swinging (see chapter 3), will give a harmonious, integrating sensation of the whole body moving and help reinforce awareness of whole body weight (Sherborne, 1990). Veronica Sherborne also set particular store on developing children's *awareness of the floor* in movement work in order to develop their confidence of the whole body moving in relation to their base. Direct contact of the body against the surface will also give indirect feedback on body image – the body as a whole, as well as specific parts.

Awareness of the floor

Sherborne (1990) advocated movement experiences to develop motor abilities on the floor initially, gradually working up to standing, 'flight' and balancing on a narrow base. She considered that this principle should run through every movement and dance session and also influence longer-term planning. Children need to be helped towards having sufficient confidence to trust their weight to the floor; indicators would be a relaxed head, arms and feet flopping outwards. By learning to manage their weight close to the floor first, the premise is that they will then stand, run and jump more confidently. For reasons of safety, too, children need to learn to fall and roll over, relaxing the shoulders against the floor.

- Sliding on stomach or back, with or without hands and/or feet to help (see figure 4.1)

Figure 4.1: Sliding on stomach

- Wriggling on stomach or back, with or without hands and/or feet to help
- Crawling on hands and knees
- Spinning on front, back or side (crossing over legs), emphasise slapping floor with hands and feet
- 'Rag dolls': lying on floor, prone or supine (maximum contact with floor); carer or children in turn to step in and out of splayed limbs; carer may test how floppy limbs are by supporting above joints, so that child 'lets go' of tension
- Rolling: child lies on side on floor, and falls on to back (encourage to relax and flop); child learns to initiate a roll with different parts of the body leading (shoulder, knee, etc.); child rolls and relaxes successively; child stiffens body and rolls as a log; child rolls and relaxes, alternating stiff/relaxed; child rolls without arms, legs or head touching the floor ('firecracker'); child rolls as one with adult; children roll each other in pairs (pushing hips and shoulders); rolling in pairs (clasping hands or feet, stretching out complete body length)
- Falling: child lies on side, and falls onto back; child sits on floor, rolls back on to shoulders and up onto hips again; child spins then falls, sits,

falls to one side, rolls on to back, sits up from opposite side (see figure 4.2); child falls from all fours ('hedgehog'), melts into floor, rolls, and comes up onto all fours; child falls from kneeling (rolls over); child falls from standing (rolls over); child jumps over partner on all fours, rolls and stands up again

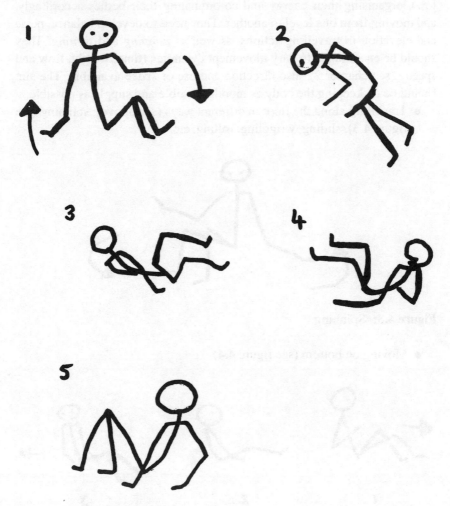

Figure 4.2: Spinning – falling – rolling

- Growing and shrinking again from little to big shapes: stretching along floor or vertically; making shapes in twos, threes or more; moving or travelling in a line or circle that grows and collapses

Locomotion skills

Developing children's awareness of the floor will enable them to manage their weight in relation to their base more confidently. Children need to explore different ways of *travelling* on a range of levels (high, medium and low), organising their energy and co-ordinating their bodies accordingly, and moving from one level to another. They need to develop balance, poise and elevation in travelling actions, as well as *jumping* and *turning*. They should be encouraged to vary movement dynamics (time, weight, flow and speed – see chapter 2), also direction and use of space available. The aim should be on keeping the body as mobile, flexible and supple as possible.

- Travelling along the floor in different ways (see above): spinning (see figure 4.3), sliding, wriggling, rolling, etc.

Figure 4.3: Spinning

- Moving on bottom (see figure 4.4)

Figure 4.4: Moving on bottom

- Moving on knees: spinning, sliding, crawling
- Squatting: walking with little legs, jumping, frog jumps, bunny jumps, waddling, bouncing, etc.

- Standing: walking with stiff legs, jelly legs, bent legs, stuck together legs, etc.
- Jumping: landing and falling, using arms and knees appropriately; on one leg, both legs; different directions (forwards, backwards, sideways, around, over); including a turn (quarter, half or whole turn)
- Running and leaping: piston elbow and knee action; running and jumping, using arms to achieve elevation; galloping and skipping

Awareness of body parts

It is not sufficient simply for children to name parts of the body: to develop awareness of body parts, they have to be *experienced*. In particular, children need to develop their awareness of parts of the body they don't usually notice, especially control and fluidity of their middle as the co-ordinating link. Also their hips and knees (the weight-bearing parts of the body): control over the lower half of the body is crucial in facilitating upright locomotion and balancing. Awareness of hips and knees may be better developed initially in floor-based work, where the child is not required to balance.

The trunk or centre

It is often apparent that many people with learning difficulties are unaware of their middles, and move in an empty, disconnected way (Sherborne, 1990). It is hard for children consciously to be aware of their middle, therefore this needs to be 'fed in'; note how, across cultures, the trunk appears later in children's figure drawings, after representation of the head and limbs. Contact of the trunk against the floor, and against other people in relationship play, will foster awareness of the trunk against supportive surfaces, without the child having to worry about maintaining balance. Activities that involve tensing the trunk muscles (e.g. to resist being pushed or pulled – see chapter 3) will also reinforce awareness indirectly of the centre. Fluidity of the trunk (as indicated through flexibility, and ability to pull into mid-line and remain curled up) will enable children to learn from bodily experiences – messages will not pass through a rigid trunk. It is possible for wheelchair-users also to develop this flexibility, by creeping along the floor, curving the spine to bend from side to side.

An 'educated trunk' indicates the child can move with free flow, flexibility and a high degree of body knowledge, and awareness of how to transfer weight through the body in an economic and fluent way. (Sherborne, 1990, p. 50)

- Press, pat or tickle the child's back or stomach in relationship play
- Contact of the trunk against the floor in locomotion: sliding, creeping, wriggling, spinning, rolling, etc.
- Somersaulting: forwards or backwards, over carer's shoulder (see figures 3.7, 3.10)
- 'Parcels': curling up tightly, sitting or kneeling; resisting being opened; maintaining shape if lifted or carried
- Tensing activities: pushing/pulling in pairs (rocks, tent-pegged, rolling partner, sliding partner, engines, etc – see chapter 3)
- 'Friar Tuck' walks: walking along, pushing out stomach
- Jiving and twisting dance actions

Weight-bearing parts of the body

Knees

The knees are half-way between the centre and the periphery, and therefore they can be seen more easily! They are vital in maintaining balance, and for acting as 'shock absorbers' for controlling standing, walking, jumping, bouncing, landing, stability, changing direction, etc. Children often enjoy their expressive potential.

- Child to sit in front of carer on floor, carer to: pat, bend, tickle, stretch, rub child's knees; feel knobbly bits, squidgy bits, underneath bits ('knee pits'?!)
- Sit in circle, percussive drumming on knees; listen to different sounds (see figure 4.5)

Figure 4.5: Percussive drumming on knees

- Sit in circle, 'disappearing and reappearing knees': show initiative in pretending to raise and lower knees at different speeds; e.g. by winding imaginary handles, pulling knees up and down in different ways, blowing them, pulling and releasing 'magic strings', etc.
- Take weight onto knees: sliding, spinning, crawling along; 'caterpillar': opening and closing to propel oneself along the floor on elbows and knees
- Squat on little legs: waddling, bouncing (knees bent)
- Wide knees: walking with wide, low slung gait
- 'Growing' knees: knees bent, pushing knees in and watching the body extend to conventional standing position
- High knees: exaggerated walking (bend knee up to chin, to ear); running, jumping, galloping, skipping (against gravity, how high are knees?)
- Expressive knees: funny walks, knee leading high, low, in different directions, etc.; jelly legs, stiff knees, melting knees, stuck together knees, etc.
- Jumping: bouncing child between two supporting carers (see figure 3.13), emphasising bending knees on landing, and tucking up knees while in the air; frog jumps (leaping forwards, sideways, knees to chin, knees bent); bunny jumps (tuck up knees to chin and to right and left); vaulting (bringing up knees to help jump, hands leaning on carer's back on all fours (see figure 3.14)
- Balancing: partners face each other, grasping forearms, bend knees to achieve state of balance (see figure 3.18)
- 'Against' relationships (see chapter 3): pushing and pulling activities, directing strength to protect knees (rocks – figure 4.6, tent-pegged, etc.); emphasis on using knees to facilitate strong and secure, stable position

Figure 4.6: 'Rocks': focusing on knees to push

Hips

These are difficult to see, although are central to the body and the heaviest body part. Good management of the hips is crucial whenever the centre of gravity is lowered; this is required in many sports, but also in dance – for example, Jazz and many African dance steps. Without good balance of the hips over the heels there will be lack of control of body weight.

- Rocking, balance on hips in sitting position: fall back on to shoulders and roll up again; swing from side to side, rolling on hips, bringing up arms in extended action
- Spinning on bottoms, without arms and legs touching the floor
- Spinning and falling (see above, figure 4.2)
- Walking on bottoms (in and out of circle, around room, etc.)
- Shuffling on bottoms (play 'chase' on bottoms!)
- Lifting and bouncing hips from sitting, supporting weight on hands and feet
- Crab walking: hips off ground, walking on hands and feet, backwards and sideways
- Bridges: making an arch (prone or supine) for partner to crawl underneath (see figure 4.7)
- Somersaults: forwards and backwards, over partner's shoulder (see figures 3.7, 3.10); carer supports pelvic girdle, child experiences hips touching ground and spine curling
- 'Bunny' or crouch jumps: squatting, taking weight on the hands, then lifting hips into the air
- Vaulting: carer makes steady 'horse' on hands and knees, child places hands on carer's hips and uses carer for support, as he or she jumps, lifting own hips high (see figure 3.14)
- Balancing: partners face each other and bend knees, feet apart, hips over heels, gripping each other by wrists (see above)

Peripheries

Children's awareness of their peripheral body parts will enhance their ability to use their body expressively. For example, hands are particularly important for developing control and sublety in use of *gesture*. Both hands and feet at times will be the point of contact of the dancer with the floor, and therefore are crucially important for supporting the body and in managing transfer of weight.

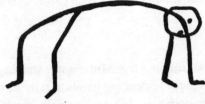

Figure 4.7: 'Bridges'

Feet

- Walking on carer's feet: child stands on carer's feet, whilst carer walks around, holding child
- Sitting in circle: tickling, rubbing, slapping feet together and on the floor; listening to noises feet make (loud, soft, etc.); tapping, slapping different parts of the foot on the floor (toes, heels, soles, sides); quick/slow movements with feet (e.g. toes disappearing, wiggling, separating toes, talking toes with person next to you, feet play in pairs, etc.)
- Moving along the floor, using feet, then not using feet to aid locomotion: sitting on bottom, propelling backwards by planting feet firmly on ground and pushing; sitting on bottom, and shuffling or waddling with legs extended, forwards and backwards; pulling

oneself along on stomach or back, using only arms (not feet) to aid mobility

- Moving on feet: toes–middle bit–heels–sides of feet; different directions; walking, sliding, hopping; big steps, little steps; exaggerated walking, toes–middle bit–heels and heels–middle bit–toes
- Jumping: land on feet; teach how to land: (land on toes–middle bit–heels)
- Moving partner using feet: pushing along; rolling over
- Shared balances: shoulder stand with partner, feet in contact, to make an arch

Hands

- Sitting in circle: rubbing legs with hands; shaking hands out, attempt to shake hands away; extending hands to star, then clench (repeat fast, then slow); chopping, slicing actions with hands in the air; working fingers individually (fast then slow); drumming hands on floor: fists, flat of hands, backs of hands, knuckles, nails; scampering 'spider' hands on floor; 'old person's hands', scratching along floor; gentle hands, stroking, looking at hands, looking after hands; catching other hand; following finger tips, where can hand go?; extending to partner (follow partner's hand)
- Transferring weight onto hands: sitting, rock from side to side, taking weight onto hands (develop into a large swinging action); bottom shuffling, leaning onto hands to aid movement; moving to crawling, take weight on hands and knees; vaulting, lean onto hands resting on carer's back (see figure 3.14)
- Using hands to move: sliding on stomach, back (using hands to help, then *not* using hands); spinning with/without hands (slap hands on floor as spin round); walking on bottoms (using hands, then *not* using hands)

Other body parts

Awareness of other body parts will contribute to children's expressive potential and to achieving poise, balance and elevation in movement. For example, appropriate facial expression will communicate meaning. Greater awareness of the back will enable children to maintain body shape. Using the elbows to assist movement will enable children to transfer weight onto their hands; also to achieve greater elevation above the ground when jumping.

Face

- Feeling own face with hands; feeling partner's face with hands (eyes open, eyes closed)
- Experimenting with wide eyes/closed eyes, wide mouth/closed mouth
- Stretching mouth, noise out of mouth?
- Experimenting with masks (i.e. *no* facial expression apparent, what can we tell from bodily expression alone?)

Elbows

- Sitting position: touch elbows on knees; touch elbows to opposite knee (see figure 4.8); rub, tickle elbows with/without partner

Figure 4.8: Touching elbow to opposite knee

- Punch elbows up into the air – whirr round and round
- Elbows to aid locomotion: 'engine' running (bringing up elbows to help action); jumping (bring elbows to help jump, extend to jumping and turning round); walking (join elbows together and pull apart); spinning (elbow to lead the spin); crawling on knees and elbows; caterpillar creeping (tucking up and extending body on knees and elbows)

Back

- Sitting: feel back (spine, knobbly bits, wobbly bits); feeling partner's back; sitting back to back, feeling partner's back through own back!
- From sitting: curling up and uncurling back, stretching from closed to open shape along the floor, or upwards to standing; tipping off balance, maintaining curled up back
- 'Parcels': child curls up tightly and maintains curled up shape whilst carer lifts elsewhere (see figure 3.22)
- Moving on backs in different ways (sliding, wriggling, spinning), using/not using hands; partners to slide each other on backs, gripping by wrists or ankles (see figure 3.15)

- Rolling: relaxing back on floor as partners roll each other
- Partners sit back to back: giving 'engine' ride to each other (see above); pushing against each other; counter balance: standing up and sitting down again; leaning on partner's back and relaxing
- 'Horse': child lies prone or supine across the back(s) of carer(s) (see figure 3.5)
- 'Vault': jumping by leaning on partner's back for support, partner on all fours (see figure 3.14)
- 'Tunnel'/'bridge': line of carers on all fours, next to one another, child to slide or wriggle through tunnel, or across backs

Moving in space

The underlying premise of the movement experiences described thus far is that developing awareness of the body and possible ways of moving will promote confidence in mobility generally. This feeling of being at ease in one's body, however, needs to be extended to the environmental *space*: recognising how to use and move through that space with confidence (Hill, 1991). This necessitates children becoming familiar with their *personal space* (the area immediately surrounding the body – reachable by extending the arms above, behind and around). They will also need to become familiar with *general space*: this involves moving the body into a different place. Contrasting experiences of moving in general space, but returning to the security of personal space, will help foster confidence in using the area available. For example, confidence may develop initially through movement experiences that begin close to the teacher: such as all sitting squashed up close, then moving away and back again (e.g. shuffling backwards to the edge of the room, then in to the middle again, on cue from the teacher).

The kind of relationship play experiences described in this chapter and previously in chapter 3 will also engender confidence in negotiating space, through helping to promote children's spatial understanding of themselves in relation to others. Making shapes and structures for one another to explore will reinforce active learning of prepositional vocabulary – over, under, through, around, next to, beside, in front of, behind, etc. Also, children are challenged to adapt their body shape, as they adjust to wriggle through spaces available or to maintain a structure for their partner to explore.

Children need to become aware of possible *directions*: forwards/backwards, high/low and side to side. The most natural direction is to move forwards;

children may need to be encouraged to experiment with trying ways of travelling in a different direction, such as moving backwards, sideways or round and round. Contrasts in *levels* will help focus this awareness: for example, moving from high to low, by leaping (extending the arms to reach upwards above the head), then falling and rolling on the floor. Contrasts in levels and directions may be reinforced also in partner or group work, where children are required to make shapes or movement patterns, in experiences that involve standing, kneeling, sitting or lying down.

As children become more confident in their movement so they may be encouraged to design pathways through space, and to trace shapes with hands or feet. Peter Slade (1977) indicated certain shapes, which he maintained were a universal feature of 'child dance' (see figure 4.9), based on the notion of movement being a 'journey' through space. He noted how any roomful of children dancing in their own way will tend to go round anti-clockwise; he attributed this to the majority of the population being right-footed rather than to any great mystical significance, however! The work of Chris Athey (1990) also suggests children may have preferred movement patterns, based on their particular schema, which will influence the way they negotiate their space (see chapter 1). Athey (1990) maintains that this schema persists from its sensori-motor beginnings, through to the development of conceptual thought. It may be a moot point, therefore, to what extent children's preferred pathways should be nurtured or extended, and the extent to which children should be urged to explore alternative patterns.

Gradually children may be encouraged to use a range of actions to negotiate their chosen 'route' through the space (e.g. jumping, rolling, leaping, etc.); also with particular parts of the body leading – for example, the top of the arm, or back of the shoulder. They may develop more complex actions by combining movements (e.g. skipping with opening and closing arms). Children may improve the quality of their movement through greater flexibility (bending, stretching and twisting) and contrasts in tension. They may work at smooth transitions between actions and greater awareness of posture. Also, leaning, inclining and over-balancing may give momentum to the next movement and enrich that movement by varying shape and size, as well as direction and level. Proximity to other dancers may give particular significance to a dance: for example whether moving away from, towards, to surround, near to, or far from one another, etc.

Children need to develop the full range of options on how to use space purposefully, so that ultimately this may be harnessed within dance to convey meaning or to create impact. Chapter 5 will consolidate a developmental framework in which to foster the development of children's understanding and use of movement for expression and impression in dance.

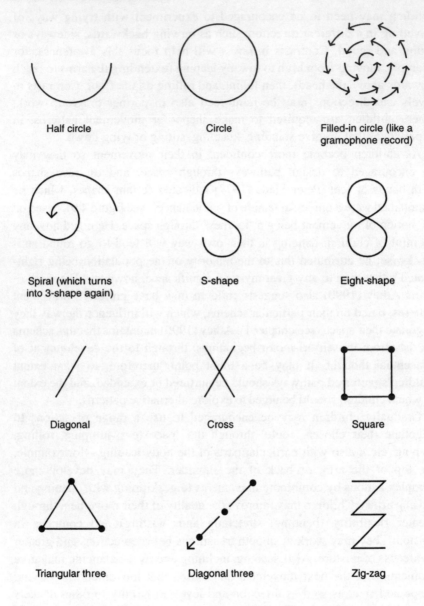

Half circle   Circle   Filled-in circle (like a
                                     gramophone record)

Spiral (which turns   S-shape   Eight-shape
into 3-shape again)

Diagonal   Cross   Square

Triangular three   Diagonal three   Zig-zag

Figure 4.9: Basic 'Child Dance' shapes – after Peter Slade (1977)

CHAPTER 5

Moving into Dance

Planning educational dance should be driven by the need to develop children's understanding and use of the elements of dance (see chapter 2) – the means by which movement may be given significance. Chapters 3 and 4 have indicated movement experiences which may provide opportunities in which the elements may be explored. This chapter presents a scheme of work across the Key stages (summarised in figure 5.1), with indication of developmentally appropriate movement experiences to address the elements of dance. This may assist in devising movement and dance work, to support teachers in meeting the requirements of the National Curriculum (see figure 1.1). An example of a lesson ilustrates how movement may be taken into dance in its narrower sense, in which children may learn to select and order movements into a sequence. Planning for dance will receive fuller consideration in chapter 6.

Developing movement skills for dance

This section outlines priority movement themes at different stages that may form the focus for a developmental scheme of work for dance. If children are to 'learn how to do dance whilst doing it', implicit is the notion that their potential 'readiness' for using the elements of dance will vary at different stages. Within any teaching group, there may be children at different stages in their movement development; children may vary too in their ability to work with particular elements. This will necessitate the teacher differentiating movement work accordingly, matching movement experiences to meet a range of individual needs. Many pupils with learning disabilities will be working at a level below their chronological age. It is important that the *context* ('theme for the children') in which *content* ('theme for the teacher') is presented respects their real ages in terms of

66 MAKING DANCE SPECIAL

PROGRESSION IN DANCE

	Pre/Lower Key Stage 1 ('Emergent') –developing awareness of movement possibilities	Upper Key Stage 1 ('Expressive') –developing control over strength and coordination
Body (what?)	• Whole body – big/little contrasts • Focusing on body parts in movement – hands, feet, elbows, knees, bottom, tummy • Whole body movement through space	• Transferring weight on to different body parts • Falling – managing body weight in relation to floor
Actions (what?)	• Travelling in different ways along the ground e.g. on back, stomach • Experience of bending, stretching, twisting • Basic actions: jumping, turning, going, stopping	• Balancing on different body parts • Performing actions with control e.g. pounce, explosion, twirling, spiralling, etc.
Space (where?)	• Exploring directions – forwards, backwards, sideways • Exploring extreme contrasts in levels – high, low • Moving in general and personal space ('close to')	• Exploring pathways on ground, in air (simulating flight, falling) • Exploring space with speed, direction • Exploring a range of levels (high to low)
Dynamics (how?)	• Awareness of ebb/flow of movement – going, stopping • Holding tension (e.g. to stretch) and letting go (shaking out, relaxing) • Exploring contrasts in speed: fast, slow movement	• Exploring contrasts in direct/flexible movement • Exploring contrasts in free (abandoned)/bound (contained) movement
Relationships (why? when? with whom?)	• 'WITH'/RECEIVING: being contained, supported e.g. cradled, rocked etc. • SHARED: exploring shapes made by others, see-saws with adult/older peer • AGAINST: pushing/pulling against older peers or adults	• 'WITH': exerting energy to support partner e.g. rolling, sliding, spinning them; trusting partner • SHARED: committing mutual weight with another e.g. see-saw, counterbalances • AGAINST: developing stability – resist being pushed/pulled by adult
Choreography	• Exploring spontaneous responses to music/accompaniment • Teacher-led dance between moments of silence • Associating sound with movement • Contributing choices and decisions	• Ordering actions to make simple sequences in solo dance • Following teacher-led narrative/story in movement • Fitting sequence/pattern to accompaniment (including simple traditional steps) • Using pictures or symbols to script a dance
Appraising dance	• Developing action-word vocabulary and feelings words • Recalling dance – developing vocabulary • Reacting and responding spontaneously to a dance	• Recalling and describing what they did • Developing imaginative responses • Watching others – peers as well as professional dance — and commenting

Figure 5.1: A developmental programme for movement and dance

Lower Key Stage 2 ('Impressive') –refining movement quality in expression to/with others	Upper Key Stage 2/3 ('Communicative') –using sensitivity in movement for expression and for creating impression
• Body shapes – combining to make group shapes • Awareness of the trunk as coordinating link • Faces – expression • Leading actions, initiated by different body parts e.g. top of arm, back of shoulder	• Open/closed body shapes • Awareness of posture • Flexibility and fluency in links between movements
• Holding stillness • Gesture e.g. pointing, reaching, nodding • Improving poise, elevation, control in basic and more complex actions • Inclining, leaning • Combining actions – e.g. coordinating hands and feet	• Smooth transitions between actions, shapes • Performing complex/combined actions • Improving quality through flexibility and contrasts in tension • Overbalancing to give momentum to the next movement
• Exploring personal space (close to) • Exploring shared space (general) • Tracing shapes with hands and feet on a range of levels • Using actions along pathways e.g. leaping, rolling	• Enriching movement by varying use of space • Designing pathways, using personal/general space
• Exploring contrasts in tension: firm/fine movement • Adjusting tension to achieve subtlety • Using rhythm/body sound as accompaniment to movement and to create patterns in dance	• Using contrasts in dynamics to give meaning and signifcance • Relating dynamics to music/accompaniment, adjusting/adapting movements accordingly • Using elements in combination
• 'WITH': using fine touch in relation to others e.g. to cradle, rock them as 'carer'; co-operating in groups • SHARED: developing balances/shapes/actions in 3s, 4s; adjusting strength to partner a younger child • AGAINST: developing stability – resist being pushed/pulled by peer	• Using relationships in harmony or opposition to give meaning and significance e.g. lift, lower, support, contain, push, pull others • Developing contrasts in moving near/far, approaching/retreating, surrounding • Using movements that match, contrast or are in canon, varied group numbers, shapes
• Devising simple solo/partner dances with beginning – middle – end • Selecting and refining actions with contrasts • Awareness of dance to make impressions e.g. presenting to others in the class	• Using a range of stimuli to convey feelings, moods, ideas in solo/partner or group dance • Using sequences and patterns creatively (including traditional steps from a range of dance styles) • Creating simple characters • Conveying a narrative in dance
• Commenting on what they have done • Describing what the dancers did and how a dance was created • Describing how the dance made them feel	• Describing and interpreting elements of a dance • Using ideas from watching dance, for inspiration and information

their interests and sophistication – this is expanded further in chapter 6. In many instances, however, it will be possible to cross reference work to the respective chronological National Curriculum key stage, with requirements interpreted freely (see Figure 1.1).

The following scheme of work is intended to address the developmental needs of pupils working particularly within the Primary age and ability range. This includes those children functioning within the framework of the Nursery Desirable Outcomes (SCAA, 1996), as well as National Curriculum Key stages 1 and 2; content may be extended for those working into Key stage 3. Teachers are now freed to select content from across the Key stages, in order to meet the particular needs of their pupils. The starting point for planning, however, should be the Programmes of Study that match the child's chronological age, with further differentiation of activities from a lower or higher stage as required.

'Emergent' phase (pre/lower Key stage 1)

This phase is equivalent to the 'scribbling' stage in art and is characterised by children's emerging awareness of movement possibilities.

The body
At this stage, children need to become aware of their whole body shape – contrasts of growing and shrinking into big and little shapes. Movement work should concentrate especially on developing awareness and flexibility of the trunk through experiences of bending, stretching and twisting. Focusing on specific body parts as movement themes for a lesson, additionally, will foster children's awareness of their weight-bearing body parts (knees, hips) in particular, and also their peripheral body parts and their expressive potential (elbows, hands, feet).

Actions
In particular, movement work at this stage should address children's mobility skills and their physical development. It should concentrate on experiences of the whole body moving along the ground (wriggling, sliding, rolling, etc.), and in the basic travelling actions: jumping, turning, going and stopping. Movement work should start low, with considerable time devoted to experiences on the floor, in order to develop children's awareness of and confidence in their base.

Space
Children may begin to explore directionality in moving: backwards and sideways as well as forwards. Also, to develop a basic awareness of high level contrasted with low level movement (along the floor). They may also experience moving in general as well as personal space: starting close to (e.g. huddled near the teacher), moving away, and returning to a 'safe area'.

Dynamics
Children may begin to develop their basic understanding of contrasts in speed: fast, sudden movement, in comparison with slow, sustained movement. They may also begin to experience holding tension (e.g. to stretch the body as high as possible), then letting it go (e.g. shaking and wiggling the body). Discovering ebb and flow of movement in this way will begin to heighten their awareness of dynamics in movement.

Relationships
Children need to become familiar with contact with others. At first they may find it easier to experience *receiving 'with' relationships*, where they are contained or supported (e.g. rocked, swung, slid, etc). This may need to be adult- (or older peer-) intensive at this stage: the children may not have sufficient social maturity or sensitivity ('fine touch') to be able to take charge of another responsibly. Same age peers may be able to begin cradling one another, however (perhaps as a calming finish to a session), provided partnerships are organised judiciously.

Children at this stage may be able to engage in *reciprocating 'shared' relationships* with an adult or older child who is able to adjust his/her own weight sensitively for the child (e.g. to see-saw). They may begin to explore shapes made by peers, however, and work towards engaging in a see-saw with a friend whom they trust.

Children may begin to pitch their energy in *controlling 'against' relationships* by taking charge of an adult (even co-operating with one another) to roll over an adult. They may not yet have sufficient social maturity, nor sufficient control over the energy they require against a smaller vulnerable physical frame, to be able to exert such force responsibly in relation to a peer.

'Expressive' phase (upper Key stage 1)

This phase should focus on children developing and consolidating control over their strength and co-ordination, to use their body expressively with growing confidence.

The body

Movement experiences should continue to foster children's awareness of parts of their body involved in that movement, and continue to reinforce awareness of the whole body moving (or being moved). Children may be offered opportunities to become adept at transferring their weight onto different body parts – moving from one kind of movement into another. In particular, movement work should aim to consolidate children's ability to manage their weight in relation to the floor: falling and rolling from different levels, relaxing the shoulders on the ground, 'giving in to their weight'.

Actions

Children need to develop their poise and elevation in basic actions: holding stillness in balances on different body parts, and greater control and co-ordination in jumping, turning, and travelling in different ways. They may be encouraged to perform actions with increasing sensitivity, adjusting their force and weight accordingly – e.g. pouncing, twirling, spiralling, stalking, etc.

Space

Children may be encouraged to work in more general space: to develop a sense of security in moving away from others and working in self-imposed boundaries. Some pupils may experience potential conflict over using general space with respect for others; they may find the idea of moving as if surrounded by an imaginary bubble helpful (Hill, 1991). They may explore space with contrasting speed and direction (forwards, backwards, sideways). Also, explore pathways on the ground and in the air (e.g. simulating flight and falling), transferring and managing their weight with increasing confidence as they move between levels.

Dynamics

With children's developing confidence in using personal and general space, it is appropriate for them to focus particularly on experiencing contrasts between 'direct' and 'flexible' pathways. Also the feeling of tense, constrained, 'bound' movement, contrasting with abandoned, 'free-flowing' movement through space.

Relationships

Children's developing ability to engage in social play may be harnessed in movement experiences: trusting to a peer in receiving 'with' relationships, to be slid, rolled, spun, etc. Similarly, the 'caring' partner may be required to exert energy sensitively to support or contain others weight.

Children may be capable, too, of committing mutual weight with a peer in *reciprocating 'shared' relationships*, concentrating and adjusting their strength sensitively in relation to their partner to engage in see-saws or counter-balances.

Children may become more consciously aware of developing their own sense of stability at this stage, through *controlling 'against' relationships*, where they are required to test their strength. For example, they may resist being pushed or pulled off their base by an adult in movement experiences that test their ability to 'stick tight' to the floor. Same age peers may not have sufficient social responsibility yet to engage in such 'mock battles'. However, the nature of the relationship may be disguised: for example, 'checking' that their friend is nice and sturdy, before using them as a vault; or two children co-operating to support a third between them, to enable their friend to do a 'giant wriggle', etc.

'Impressive' phase (lower Key stage 2)

During this phase, children should focus on refining movement quality in expression to and with others, and on encapsulating ideas in movement, with a growing awareness of the impressive impact of dance on an audience.

The body
During this phase, children may experiment with a range of body shapes, perhaps combining with peers to make group shapes. Children may need to 'revisit' movement experiences that foster awareness of the trunk (the co-ordinating link), to help improve flexibility and fluency between movements. They may begin to focus on 'leading actions': a particular part of the body initiating a movement – e.g. top of the arm, back of the shoulder, following a finger, etc. They may also focus on the face and its expressive potential in dance.

Actions
Children may become aware of the power of stillness: concentrating on maintaining a pose without fidgeting or giggling! Their growing ability to co-operate with others may enable them to harness inclining and leaning actions, perhaps overbalancing, to give momentum to the next movement. Having gained control over gross actions from the shoulder, children may begin to develop their use of gesture – subtlety in actions that do not involve

travelling, and which may carry meaning (e.g. recoil, point, nod, flinch, etc). Children may also be encouraged to perform more complex, combined actions such as co-ordinating arms and feet in travelling, or jumping and turning at the same time.

Space

Children may be encouraged to explore general and personal space in different ways, tracing shapes with hands and feet on a range of levels, or with other body parts leading. They may use actions along direct or flexible pathways – e.g. rolling, leaping, etc.

Dynamics

At this stage, it may be appropriate to focus overtly on children's awareness of contrasts in tension: firm and strong compared with fine and delicate movement. They may become more aware of how this affects the quality of an action, and be conscious of adjusting tension to achieve subtlety in their own movement.

Relationships

Children's social responsibility and control over their strength may enable them to engage in a range of relationship play movement experiences. They may be capable of sufficient 'fine touch' to partner a younger or more vulnerable peer in *receiving 'with' relationships;* they may also be capable of co-operating with peers in groups, to take charge of a peer to support, lift, lower or contain one another.

Similarly, they may be able to engage in *reciprocating shared relationships*, adjusting their weight sensitively to engage in a mutual balance with a smaller child; also to develop and maintain balances, shapes and actions in larger groupings of peers such as threes and fours.

They may have sufficient social maturity to engage in 'mock battles' with peers, testing their partner's ability to remain strong, secure and stable, by pushing or pulling in *controlling 'against' relationships*. They may begin also to feed in this strength and sense of stability to others by partnering a more vulnerable or younger child.

'Communicative' phase (upper Key stage 2/3)

During this phase, children may now use sensitivity in movement both in responding expressively and also to create an impression: using movement intentionally for meaning with growing confidence to make a statement.

The body
Children may become particularly aware of posture at this stage: for example, how open and closed shapes may be used to give significance to an action and convey a particular emotion. They may become more aware, also, of the significance of posture to particular dance styles and traditions – low slung in jazz and African dance, compared with upright stance in north European dance (e.g. Morris dancing).

Actions
At this stage, children should focus on making smooth transitions between actions, maintaining body shapes. These actions themselves may be of varying complexity or simplicity and on a range of levels, for example, incorporating jumps and turns. Children may become more aware of improving quality of movement, through flexibility and contrasting use of tension, in order to give sensitivity to a range of actions.

Space
Children may be encouraged to design their own pathways using both personal and general space. Also, using space to enrich movement: dancing close to, far away, and with big or little movements. This may acquire particular significance in using space in relation to others: approaching, retreating, surrounding, moving towards or away from them, etc.

Dynamics
Children may become aware how using contrasts in dynamics (fast/slow, strong/light, direct/flexible, bound/free-flowing) may be harnessed in combination to create meanings in movements, for example a strong, slow movement; a light flexible sudden movement. They may relate dynamics to music or accompaniment, adjusting their movements accordingly.

Relationships
Children may now harness their energy sensitively, to lift, lower, support or contain another dancer. They may be aware how using their strength in harmony or opposition may communicate meanings. Children should be encouraged to work co-operatively in groupings of different sizes as required, and to accept working in mixed-gender groupings of peers who may not necessarily be their first-choice friends. They may begin to bring this same sensitivity in adjusting their strength in relation to others, to give the same quality to movement that does not actually involve 'hands on' contact. Children may organise movements in relation to others that match, contrast, or are in canon (performed one after the other).

Developing knowledge and understanding of dance

So how can the teacher support pupils in choosing and organising movement experiences to create dance in its narrow sense? Quite simply, children need to develop their repertoire of movement possiblities on a particular theme, from which they may then select and combine particular movements into a sequence. Dances may be constructed very simply. Essentially, dances are particular movements linked in a sequence. A possible starting-point is to think about the statement to be made through the dance. In other words, what is the *intention*: *why* is the dance being performed? What meanings are to be conveyed through movement: communication of an idea, or purely the sensation of moving in space (Allen and Coley, 1995)?

Once children have a grasp of the kind of effects they wish to create through dance they may then focus on *how* they will draw on the dance elements:

- *which* parts of the body will be involved, and its shape and size;
- *what* actions the body will do and how these actions are going to be connected (transitions);
- *where* the body will go: pathways, directions and levels in space;
- *how* the actions will be performed (fast or slow, strong or light, direct or flexible, tense or abandoned);
- *with whom or what* the dance will be performed.

A *structure* then needs to be decided; this will give the dance content unity, shape and form (Arts Council of Great Britain, 1993). Various compositional structures may be used:

- theme and variation (improvisation within a structure)
- verse and chorus (repeated pattern)
- AB (two contrasting sections)
- ABA (a dance sandwich, with a central section that contrasts with the first and last)
- ABC (three contrasting sections)
- unison, follow-my-leader
- rondo (ABACA: a 'double-decker dance sandwich', with two contrasting central sections)

According to their age and social maturity, children will vary in the extent to which they are able autonomously to devise, rehearse, refine and perform a repeatable sequence of movements in a pattern to create a dance. Teachers need to consider differentiation strategies for enabling children to choreograph – to *compose* dance; for example, level of staffing support, complexity of the structure, length of time allowed to develop a piece, etc.

(see chapter 7). Teachers need to find ways to maximise children's creative input, even if for certain children this means making choices structured by the teacher (for more detail on the role of the teacher, see chapter 7). Teachers may need to interpret positive reactions and responses to different movement experiences on behalf of those pre-verbal children and those with PMLD, as the basis for the child indicating preferred material to be the content for a dance; for example, his or her favourite ways of experiencing the action of spinning, to be linked in a sequence.

'Performance' does not necessarily mean presenting to a specially invited audience. Nevertheless, from an early age children may be helped to *understand* the visual language that is dance. Children should become used to sharing their work with others and develop confidence in *expression*, at all stages of the creative process. In this way, they may learn through observing one another and from the constructive suggestions of others; also they become accustomed to the notion that their movement can make an *impression* and be shaped to create an impact in dance. In framing questions to guide observation (Arts Council of GB, 1993), teachers should focus on:

- *what* is happening in the dance (actions, basic structure);
- *how* it is happening (use of the body, dynamics, space and relationships);
- *how* the dance makes you feel (the subjective interpretation and response).

Especially with a large class, it may not be feasible for everyone to be moving at the same time. Those children that are 'sitting out' should be given the responsibility as audience to offer constructive criticism and comments to the dancers. Children may be given specific tasks in their role as 'dance critics' (see chapter 6, section on 'Developing Active Watching'), which will not only help focus their attention better but also enable them to learn from observing one another and to develop their aesthetic *appreciation*. As already stated elsewhere, an atmosphere needs to be fostered right from the start in which children may feel confident in using movement expressively, without fear of failure or ridicule. There may be permutations on managing numbers:

- half the class dance, half observe
- half the class sit strategically within the dance space, the other half dance around them
- small groups present their work in turn
- the whole class dances together (space permitting).

'Emergent' phase (pre/lower Key stage 1)

Choreography

Children may be encouraged to respond spontaneously to music or accompaniment. Nevertheless, this needs to happen within a clear 'frame': insist on silence and stillness (as far as possible), so that children learn that movement may carry special significance – distinct from the movement that characterises everyday action. Children should learn to associate sound with movement, learning to move in sympathy with the particular accompaniment. At the most fundamental level, children with PMLD may recognise an extract of music associated with dance, and indicate through their expression that they are anticipating movement. Children may be able to perform a teacher-led, broadly improvised dance, based on a 'copy-cat' follow-my-leader principle. Selected actions may be negotiated and agreed ahead, based on movements covered in the lesson. The extent to which children are able to contribute choices and decisions to create a dance may depend on the sensitive interpretation of preferred responses and reactions to movement explored in the lesson and on the questioning skills of supporting staff (see chapter 6).

Appraising dance

Children may be encouraged to develop an action-word vocabulary and 'feelings' words for appreciating dance. Their understanding will be developed through active learning within the lesson. They should be encouraged to *use* this vocabulary, in recalling their dance and in describing the content of a dance they are watching. Even if they are unable to articulate their feelings, children's reactions to a dance may be apparent from their spontaneous responses.

'Expressive' phase (upper Key stage 1)

Choreography

Children may be encouraged to devise their own sequence of actions, to make a solo dance. For example, simply selecting their three favourite ways of moving (e.g. on their knees: see example at the end of this chapter) and practising these, until they are confident and fluent with the actions; also deciding on a clear starting and finishing position. They may show their sequence to a friend, who may offer constructive comments or suggestions on how it may be improved. Their 'dance' may be performed to percussion accompaniment, with three clearly contrasting types of sounds to indicate a change of movement; alternatively, to an extract of pre-recorded music with distinct sections.

Extending this principle, children may learn to fit their sequence to a specific accompaniment: teacher's percussion may be more flexible than a pre-recorded extract of music. This may be developed to include learning some simple steps from a particular dance style or tradition, and fitting these steps to the basic pulse and structure of the accompaniment. Similarly, children may fit a routine to an accompaniment, in order to convey a teacher-led narrative or story in movement. Picture cues as a script may help as an additional prompt to recall sections of a dance.

Appraising dance
Children should be encouraged to recall and describe what they did to create their dance. It may be that they are asked to watch their partner perform a dance, and to be ready to describe what he or she did. Children should be encouraged, too, to develop imaginative responses to a dance they have watched, legitimating the subjective response: how a dance made them feel.

'Impressive' phase (lower Key stage 2)

Choreography
Children's developing social skills may enable them to devise simple partner dances as well as solos. These should have a clear beginning, middle and end, and involve children collaborating to select and refine actions. One way of achieving this is for each partner to select one favourite action from the lesson, then the pair agree the third one, combining them into a sequence. In refining their dance, they may need to be reminded of the range of dynamics and contrasts in use of space that may make their dance more interesting; also, how they are to perform their chosen actions in relation to each other. It may be helpful for the teacher to interject a challenge, to specify requirements for the dance. For example: the dance is to include a change of level, one dancer moving whilst the other is still, a moment where dancers move towards then away from one another, etc.

Appraising dance
Children may be encouraged to comment on how they devised their dance. Similarly, when watching dance they may be asked to comment on *what* the dancer(s) did, and *how* they did it (i.e. comments related to the dynamics of dance and the use of space); also how dancer(s) moved in relation to one

another. Additionally, how the dance made them feel – the subjective impact and interpretation an individual may have as audience.

'Communicative' phase (upper Key stage 2/3)

Choreography

During this phase, children may be encouraged to work from a range of stimuli (see chapter 6) to convey feelings, moods, or ideas. They may devise solo, partner or group dances, possibly to convey a narrative. They may create simple characters and capture the essence of characterisation particularly through using gestures and *dynamics* in combination to give movement quality (see chapter 2). Dances should not be too complicated: it is better to focus on a limited number of actions to be performed in a sequence (possibly repeated several times over), with children aiming to execute this as fluently as possible. Similarly, they may learn prescribed sequences of steps (including those from some traditions and particular dance styles) and be encouraged to work with them creatively: to choreograph an original routine using the steps, performing dance patterns in relation to one another.

Appraising dance

In watching dance, as above, children should describe and interpret a dance by analysing it according to the way the elements have been used. They should be encouraged to justify their observations; for example, what made the dance 'good'? What could have made it more effective? In particular, children may appreciate the way choreographers use contrasts to make dance effective; they may use ideas to inform and inspire their own work.

Dance in action

There follows an example of how *movement* may be taken into *dance* within a lesson. A rationale is offered alongside the respective movement activities, to clarify objectives. Planning for dance will be considered more fully in the next chapter.

It will be seen here, however, that a dance lesson structure essentially has four stages:

1. *establishing the theme*
   - theme for the children (e.g. a stimulus: 'lesson about balloons')
   - theme for the teacher (movement objective, based on the elements of dance, e.g. the action of bouncing)

2. *warming up*
   - experiences of bending, stretching, twisting, related to the movement content of the lesson
3. *development and exploration*
   - experimenting with movement ideas and possibilities related to the movement objective(s), in experiences that offer in-depth awareness
4. *selecting and creating*
   - choosing and combining material into phrases or sequences
   - teacher or pupil-led
   - practising and perfecting
   - presenting and reflecting

Example: Awareness of knees

The following lesson is suitable across the age and ability range, although developmentally young children may find some of the movement experiences challenging and require specific support. A full range of movement experiences is included, however, to indicate possible activities addressing the movement theme in question ('awareness of knees', weight-bearing body parts). Clearly, there are far too many activities just for one lesson – there is sufficient material here to last over several sessions or a module of work. It is better to explore material in-depth, rather than rush through to complete the lesson in one.

The implication is that the same theme may be revisited, with new challenges introduced over time. For example, the 'dance' section indicates a teacher-led 'follow-me' dance, a simple way of developing a solo dance, and more challenging partner and group tasks for older children. Material may be revisited in future lessons: 'awareness of knees' re-presented in other contexts, so that children may improve their confidence and skill in familiar movement experiences.

Example: Awareness of knees

Objectives:
- awareness of knees
- using energy in harmony ('with' relationships)

Activity	Movement rationale
establishing the theme	
• sit in circle: draw attention to people sitting in different ways, and position of their knees	raising awareness of knees and how they help in movement
• tickle and rub knees, also neigbour's knees	
• percussive drumming on knees (make a range of sounds around the circle)	awareness of others, appreciating individual contributions; establishing 'the group'
warming up	
• sit with knees tucked up (pull into mid-line, put chin on knees	flexion exercise (bending)
• tip gently to rock forwards and backwards, side to side	maintaining shape, tensing to foster flexibility of the trunk
• blow knees away, find different ways to bring knees up again (imaginary handles, string, etc!)	stretching of the limbs; contrast in speed (awareness of dynamics)
• sit with legs out straight, turn body to look behind, one way, then the other	rotation exercise, flexibility of the trunk
• from sitting: hug knees, slowly uncurl into a stretch	flexion and extension exercises
• from kneeling: curl up tightly ('parcels'), slowly uncurl into a stretch along the ground;	testing children's ability to maintain their shape (try to undo, or carry to another part of the circle)
• repeat, stretching upwards	maintaining balance, moving up from the floor (wide base) to standing (narrow base)
development and exploration	
• sit in circle: use knees to help propel backwards, to make a big circle, move in again to the middle	easing children into moving from personal into general space
• huddle up close (tuck up knees), move backwards as fast as possible using knees but no hands to help	awareness of knees in aiding mobility on floor
• repeat, shuffling and waddling on bottoms, in and out of the circle	
• sit with knees tucked up, spin round; develop into a fall (from sitting) and roll over	practising 'giving into weight to the floor' by relaxing (letting go of tension)
• move onto knees: spin, fall and roll from kneeling	
• find different ways to travel on knees (slide, spin, crawl, waddle, etc.); copy children's ideas	encouraging originality, praising individuals learning from one another
• hands and knees: bring up one knee at a time to chin, then extend leg behind (look round at knee)	transferring weight onto hands
• hands and knees: bunny jumps, taking weight on hands	
• move onto little legs: find different ways to travel; copy children's ideas (bounce, waddle, frog jumps, etc.)	awareness of knees in aiding low level actions
• find partner: help each other to walk on little legs	
• grow legs: walk with stiff legs, teach legs to walk (bend knees!)	developing confidence on narrower base

- walk with jelly legs, stuck together knees
- silly walks, where can knee take you?
- practise high knees: walk, bringing up knees; break into a trot, then put in a leap
- with partner: partner to become vault (on hands and knees), practise jumping (tuck up knees)

expressive potential of knees
knees to give balance and support
knees to aid high level actions; jumping

practising elevation; trusting weight to partner
'with' relationships: partners supporting, being

Activity	Movement rationale
• partner to stand with arms outstretched, offering support to forearms: practise jumping	firm and stable
• partners face each other, grip by wrists: move from standing to sitting, bending knees; hold balance half way	'shared' relationship, mutually adjusting energy
• partner to curl up: practise jumping over them, tucking up knees to gain height; develop into a pounce and roll over, coming up onto knees	developing trust and confidence
• in threes: two help third to jump (supporting above wrist and elbow), tucking up knees, and bending knees to land; develop into a low level supported wriggle	developing elevation co-operating in larger groupings
• in groups of four or more: go on hands and knees to make human tunnel (or bridge), child to lie across backs, wriggle across backs, or crawl through the tunnel	developing co-operation, to maintain structure

selecting and creating
- teacher-led 'follow-me' dance to accompaniment with clearly contrasting sections or prompting jerky or smooth-flowing responses; children to take turns to be the leader, start on the floor (sitting in circle), and move to kneeling, then standing and travelling

teacher building on cues from the children, and their initiatives, to support them in making choices and decisions over preferred content

- *or* solo dance: choose three favourite ways of travelling, using knees to help, with contrasts in level: start with low level, move to medium level (little legs), move to high level (favourite silly walk); show actions to partner, aiming to change from one movement to the next smoothly; have a clear starting and finishing position;

encouraging awareness of importance of knees in mobility at different levels

developing fluidity and flexibility in transition

'shaping' movement between stillness

individual solo dance, to three contrasting percussion accompaniment – perform as half-and-half dance, so that partners may observe one another

matching movement to accompaniment
partner to describe what their partner did, and what bit they liked best

- *or* in pairs, choose three knee actions (one from each person, and the third negotiated); work out how to perform the actions in relation to one another

developing co-operation and negotiation; also the power of use of space to make a statement, and awareness of contrasts

- *or* choreographing a routine in threes or fours: three contrasting sections based on using the knees in movement, to be performed in relation to one another (actions that match, contrast or are in canon); moving towards, away or around one another; tracing pathways in space, and on a range of levels etc.

extending co-operation and negotiation skills; using space and awareness of movement in relation to others to make a statement

CHAPTER 6

Planning for Dance

This chapter looks at the planning process for dance. It starts with developing movement work with children, literally from small beginnings. Principles for planning are then developed, with consideration for structuring a lesson and taking movement work into dance. This may include working from a range of stimuli and using accompaniment; also developing children's own work from watching professional dance. Issues concerned with devising modules of work are discussed, to plan for progression and continuity within and between sessions. Further sections consider in more detail strategies for developing 'active watching' and for developing work based on particular dance styles and traditions.

Beginning movement work

The physical conditions of the room will affect the class; ideally it needs to be warm, light and airy. It will be apparent by now that floor-based work is important at all age and ability levels: developing confidence in movement through familiarity and knowledge of one's base, but also learning to manage one's weight in relation to the floor. Consideration of the floor surface itself should not be under-estimated. It needs to be clean, slightly slippery, and not too cold to the touch. The ideal is a sprung, splinter-free wooden floor; concrete screeds do not yield and may jar children's legs when jumping. Schools often have vinyl floorings, which are cold underfoot and therefore not so friendly, although they do facilitate sliding and spinning activities. Carpeting and mats, while comfortable for one-to-one relationship play, are limited for movement involving flow; watch that children do not experience carpet burns from friction with the surface. Check, too, that the floor is swept, especially if the room has previously been used over lunchtime!

Ensure that staff and children are wearing clothing that is appropriate: loose, comfortable and dignified. For safety, long hair should be tied back and jewellery and watches removed. Working in bare feet will help give grip (therefore greater safety); it will also provide maximum awareness of the floor through the feet. Depending on age or ability, work may start very small: for example, sessions that are perhaps just five to ten minutes long initially, perhaps just with one child. Sessions may be lengthened as children's ability to concentrate improves and as their involvement increases. Children may find it less threatening to work in a familiar space initially: in a corner of the classroom, perhaps on a mat, screened from the rest of the class. Being confronted with the expanses of the school hall can be very exposing – for children, as well as adults. With regard to 'child protection' issues, staff may feel more secure in developing 'hands on' work if there is always another adult present in the room.

In order to become acquainted with the movement needs of the child(ren), it may be useful initially for the the focus of dance sessions to be on relationship play (see chapter 3). Don't worry too much about the rigour of the session at first. Rather, react intuitively and spontaneously, in glorified rough-and-tumble type of activities (Nind and Hewitt, 1994). It may be preferable not to use music or accompaniment at this stage, in order to focus on the movement itself and inner sensations. Use the opportunity to make a rough base-line assessment (based on Sherborne, 1990):

- Does the child accept being supported (let you take his/her weight)?
- Does the child accept being contained?
- Does the child enjoy free-flowing movement while being supported or contained (e.g. being swung)?
- Does the child trust his or her weight to the floor (relax on it, lie down)?
- Can the child balance with another (e.g. see-saw)?
- Can the child be firm and stable (e.g. resist being pushed or pulled)?
- Can the child direct and control his or her energy (e.g. to try to push adult over)?
- Does the child have flexibility and control over the trunk (to bend, curl up)?
- Is the child aware of his or her knees – sitting (no weight) and standing (bearing weight)?
- Is the child aware of other parts of the body?
- Does the child relate to another child?
- Is the child confident in movement?
- Does the child have delicate and 'fine touch', or are actions forceful?
- Does the child have an awareness of fast or sudden movement contrasted with slow and sustained movement?
- Does the child enjoy free flowing movement or is he/she tense?
- Does the child prefer personal space that is close to or does he/she

explore general, more wide-ranging space?
- Does the child tend to move in roving pathways or follow more direct routes?

Answering this kind of check-list may indicate an individual child's priority needs for developing a control of his or her strength through relationship play experiences and for focusing on developing body awareness. For example, a child may enjoy being swung or rocked by an adult and be able to see-saw; he or she may begin to show initiative to push an adult over. The child may show some rigidity in gait, e.g. have difficulty arching the back to curl over and limited 'give' in the knees when bounced from standing. Perhaps the child tends to rush at tasks in rather a ham-fisted way, and be rather 'up-tight'.

The above movement observation may suggest a 'readiness' to co-operate with others to push or pull against an adult (e.g. to roll an adult over); to begin resisting being pushed or pulled by an adult (see chapter 3). It may be worth trying the child partnering a peer in order to see-saw, also to roll the partner over, slide or spin the partner responsibly. However, the child may not yet have sufficient maturity or control over his or her strength to engage in more overt tests of strength or 'mock battles' with a peer. The movement observation might suggest, too, a need for an intensive focus on movement experiences to foster awareness of the trunk; and to develop awareness of knees. It would appear to indicate, too, a need to work towards slower, sustained movement, with plenty of experiences using strength. This might enable the child to develop sufficient control to achieve delicacy and lightness in movement. Plenty of free-flowing experiences (harnessing the child's enjoyment of being moved through space) may enable the child to 'let go' of his or her tension.

Whether or not such assessment takes place in a one-to-one context, the teacher will need to identify the movement starting-points for all the children in the group. It may be that assessment opportunities have to be created within the context of a group session – particularly with larger classes and older or developmentally more mature pupils. The teacher will be able to 'play safe' with regard to planning a lesson for the group at first by selecting a movement theme (e.g. awareness of middles, awareness of feet, working in pairs, etc.), and working through a range of appropriate experiences (see chapters 3 and 4). As the teacher becomes more familiar with individual needs and abilities, so differentiation of activities can be tuned more finely (see below). For example, Johnny may have sufficient sensitivity and fine touch to take responsibility for a peer, whereas Susan may need to learn to relax and trust her weight to a peer, not just to an adult; so these two working together might prove a fruitful partnership for activities, where Johnny is required to roll over or cradle Susan, thus enabling both to work on their specific individual objectives.

In all movement work, the teacher will need to develop a 'Rubik's cube' mind, to retain awareness of the individual needs of all the children in the group with a view to correcting lop-sided development in all aspects of movement and dance work:

- in how they move
- in the development of their self-image
- in the development of relationships and their awareness of others.

Within the context of the group the teacher will need to plan for breadth and balance of movement experiences, given that children will demonstrate a range of needs and natural starting-points for dance (see chapter 2). It will be important to vary dynamics by contrasts in movement quality (see chapter 2), and to ensure that there is a full range of movement experiences that require bending, stretching and twisting. The implication is that over time, opportunities need to be provided that present a balance of familiar activities with appropriate new challenges. In this way, all children will be able to:

- find security and confidence in what they do best
- extend their repertoire of movement possibilities.

It is worth re-stating here some points that have been made previously. The atmosphere should be positive and enabling – fun and informal! Staff need to be fully involved – enthusiastic, and, ideally down on the floor as necessary. Initially, the teacher may need to demonstrate an activity, for instance, possible ways of moving on one's knees. However, the intention should be to feed the germ of an idea, and to encourage initiative from the children. Putting the spotlight on particular children will enable them to learn by observing one another and then trying out new possibilities. The teacher may be deliberately strategic over group dynamics; for example, praising the achievement of children whose status with their peers needs raising. Gradually, as the group becomes more confident and innovative, the teacher's role as a demonstrator may decrease. The social health and teacher-pupil relationships will benefit from a different way of relating, fostering individual achievement in a context where nobody can 'fail' (see chapter 3). This kind of atmosphere nurtured through movement work (relationship play) will stand the group in good stead when taking movement into dance.

Lesson planning for dance

The National Curriculum (DFE, 1995) states that:

Physical education should involve pupils in the continuous process of planning, performing and evaluating. This applies to all areas of activity. The greatest emphasis should be placed on the actual performance aspect of the subject... (p 2)

Translated into 'dance speak', Planning, Performing and Evaluating can be applied to the processes of Composing, Performing and Appreciating. For example (adapted from the Arts Council of GB, 1993):

	Planning	Performing	Evaluating
Composing: contrasts of speed	when should movements be fast or slow? what body parts will be involved?	different ways of moving fast or slow	when were speeds used? was it easy to be fast or slow?
Performing: a set dance	what are the significant features? e.g. stance, qualities, actions	performing the dance with attention to the significant features	how can it be improved?
Appreciating: dance expressing fear	what actions, gestures, qualities are used?	watching the dance	how were movements combined? Did it work?

Emphasis on 'performance' (confusingly in the case of dance!) is not intended to imply presentation to an audience necessarily. Rather, it is meant to suggest development and exploration of skills related to a particular idea – in this case, interpretations of a movement theme related to the elements of dance. Hence the importance of the 'development and exploration' section to the lesson (see below). That should not be compromised for the sake of rushing pupils into selecting and sequencing movements to create a dance. As already stated, it is better to continue one lesson over several sessions in order for pupils to develop work in-depth at an appropriate pace, and then be able to make much more informed choices.

The Arts Council of GB (1993) describes the dance lesson as:

...a place of exploration and investigation. At times the class may be unified, with everyone engaged in learning the same dance or movements. At other times, pupils will be working individually or in groups, discussing and negotiating ways forward, evaluating various options and reaching consensus. Every pupil should be engaged in a structured task that is relevant, challenging and achievable (para 4.9, p. 16).

As indicated at the end of chapter 5, a dance lesson structure essentially has four stages (summarised on to a lesson plan proforma – see figure 6.1):

- establishing the theme
- warming up
- development and exploration
- selecting and creating.

DANCE LESSON PLAN

Date ....   Group ....

Time ....   Staff ....

Nat. Cur. refs ....

Resources ....

ESTABLISHING THE THEME
What movement objectives (for group individuals) will the lesson address? (actions? dynamics? body parts/shape? relationships? space?). Use of a stimulus? (object? picture? story? etc.). Accompaniment? (live or recorded sounds? extract of music?).

▼

WARM-UP EXERCISES
Check mood of the group (do they need to let off steam? Do they need to be 'grounded', with small movements on the floor?). Movements 'in place' – bending, stretching, twisting from sitting, kneeling, standing, Exercises to relate to movement objectives.

▼

DEVELOPMENT AND EXPLORATION
In-depth experiences to extend possibilites relating to movement objectives: body parts, space, dynamics, relationships and actions – travelling, balancing, jumping, turning and gesture. Also to develop transfer of weight and poise (stillness).

▼

SELECTING AND CREATING
Selecting and combining material into phrases/sequences. Teacher- or group-led. Practising and perfecting – presenting and reflecting.

EVALUATION – Comments and future priorities

Figure 6.1: Lesson plan proforma for dance

Establishing the theme

Movement themes need to be selected with an overview to providing breadth and balance of experiences for the group in 'blocked' units of work in the medium term, while retaining on-going individual objectives in 'continuing' work (SCAA, 1996b). Movement themes need to be movement objectives, based on the elements of dance, e.g. the action of bouncing. This may be presented overtly to children at the start of the lesson, as in the example of the 'knees' lesson at the end of chapter 5. Children will need reinforcement of the movement theme as the lesson progresses, e.g. 'how high can your knees take you?', when experimenting with their 'silly walk'.

Alternatively, the movement theme may be presented via a stimulus. The point, however, is *not* to find a stimulus and then think of dance work based on it. Rather, planning should begin from children's movement needs, with a stimulus perhaps selected in order to clarify ideas, and make them concrete to the children. It is important to reflect children's interests or arouse children's involvement with intriguing objects and images. Movement ideas may be found by referring to real images; for example (Lowden, 1989, p.41):

Movement idea	Stimulus/image
Change	Ice melting, paper burning, leaves wilting, ink in water, screwed paper unfolding, yeast growing, water evaporating, spaghetti cooking
Dispersing and coming together	Smoke from a snuffed candle, a deflating balloon, iron filings drawn to a magnet, spilt peas, spilt water, children coming to school, blown litter, swept leaves, a vacuum cleaner
Increase and decrease	Inflating a balloon, breathing, seeds growing, folding paper, the tides, a bath filling, shadows in sunshine, a car approaching
Shape	Shells, buildings, scaffolding, rocks, paint and blots, vegetables and fruit cut in half, prickles and thorns, concave mirrors, reflections, mouths and eyes in laughter, clouds, hands
Movement	Smoke, balls rolling, water dripping, clouds forming, waves breaking, wind-blown grass, pistons and wheels, elastic, a tissue falling

An external focus, therefore, may be helpful for motivating the group and to suggest an idea. Moving things may prompt a quick immediate response; for example:

balloons   grow – shrink – float – bounce – roll – burst
bubbles   float – bounce – burst

In those two examples alone it will be seen how the same movement idea (bouncing, floating, bursting) may be revisited through different stimuli, enabling children to consolidate aspects of learning about the dance elements. From the children's point of view, however, they are 'doing dance about different things'. An object may also suggest starting or finishing positions for a dance and the maintenance of body shape ('roundness' in the two examples above). Beware the whole thing does not become too cerebral, however, with the stimulus clouding the issue of the movement intention. The point of a stimulus is to inspire movement quality, or to suggest actions or body shape. It is better then to put the stimulus to one side, and encourage different responses and avoid stereotypical ones. In other words, the stimulus should be used to select movement ideas relevant to a particular movement theme.

A stimulus, however, can also be used as something to move *with*. This can help overcome self-consciousness with certain pupils. For example, children who might be reluctant to engage in movement work in relation to others may find themselves co-operating, moving around the room keeping a balloon between them. Even so it is better at some point during the lesson to put the stimulus to one side and encourage children to move *as if* they are still working with it, in order to focus on the quality of the movement. Moving with a stimulus can also extend movement; for example, ribbons to enhance small movements of the finger.

Warming up

As already indicated in previous chapters, warm-up activities are needed to limber up the muscles. Therefore the full range of movement types needs to be covered: bending, stretching and twisting activities will allow for flexion, extension and rotation of the muscles, respectively. It is not sufficient, however, solely to prepare the body. Warm-up activities also need to prepare children for an appropriate 'mental set' required for the lesson, and to create an appropriate atmosphere. In fact, in terms of the children's attitude, 'cool down' exercises may be more suitable: to develop concentration and calm, perhaps sustained notions of time.

Warm-up exercises, therefore, should be related to the movement content of the lesson: do not keep this a secret – rather, make the movement intention of the lesson clear to the children. Warm-ups with children working towards or within Key stage 1 may have more of a 'do as I do' flavour, whereas those working towards or within Key stage 2 or beyond may be given more scope to innovate within a clear structure; for example, 'on the bang of the drum, make a shape in groups of three, four, five six'. They may be empowered with the responsibility for suggesting appropriate warm-up exercises for the group – one of the general requirements for PE in the National Curriculum (DFE, 1995, p.2).

Some examples of warm-up activities, related to particular movement themes follow.

The body
On a signal, run into a space and make a shape: (e.g.) with a particular body part nearest the ceiling, in contact with the ground, in contact with another person, in contact with a stipulated number of people, etc.

Actions
Perform actions using the knees, matching movement to eight sets of eight counts: (e.g.) bouncing knees – moving on knees – travelling using knees – stretching with knees out straight (repeat).

Space
Keep a person in mind and aim to get as near to them as possible (or as far away as possible), while having to change direction on the beat of a drum: (e.g.) moving in a straight pathway, moving in a wiggly pathway, alternating types of pathway, reducing the space available by sectioning off part of the area, travelling backwards, sideways or forwards, etc.

Dynamics
Limbering exercises that emphasise the same action performed in contrasting ways: (e.g.) slowly then quickly, holding tension (such as stretching) then shaking out, moving from high to low and vice versa (stretching along the ground, then stretching up high); performing precise actions contrasting with sinewy ones (swaying both arms from side to side, then punching the air with each arm in turn from high to low) etc.

Relationships
Mirroring a partner's actions through the hands in different ways, teacher feeding in specific directions to ensure bending, stretching and twisting

actions: (e.g.) facing one another, side by side, in front/behind one another, whilst travelling, on different levels (high/medium/low)

Development and exploration

This is the most important part of the lesson. It should involve children trying out new ideas and developing their movement vocabulary, with a view to this becoming increasingly complex. This section of the lesson will involve children experimenting with movement ideas and possibilities related to the movement objective(s) in experiences that offer in-depth awareness of the theme. Broadly speaking, with children working within Key stage 1, the content of lessons should focus particularly on developing confidence with the body as a means for non-verbal expression. Movement themes should address awareness of the whole body moving in space, and the contribution of particular body parts in facilitating movement (trunk, knees, feet, etc.); awareness too of body shape and the execution of the basic actions of travelling, jumping and turning with growing confidence, co-ordination, poise and elevation. Control of children's energy should be fostered in movement experiences that involve them pitching their strength in relation to others.

With children working in Key stage and beyond, there should be an increasing emphasis on developing their awareness of using the impressive impact of movement. Movement themes should focus on developing complexity and fluidity of actions, especially improving transitions between actions on different levels (managing weight in relation to the floor) and transferring weight onto different body parts. They should also focus on consolidating children's ability to hold stillness, maintaining their balance. Greater control of their strength should facilitate exploration of subtle movement and the use of gesture; also adjusting tension and other dynamics of a movement (e.g. speed, pathway, etc.). In particular, too, movement themes should foster co-operating and negotiating with others, through movement experiences that require them to work in groups of different sizes and with all-comers (not necessarily their first-choice friends).

Chapter 5 presented the above simplistic overview as a more detailed scheme of work to address development in children's skill, knowledge and understanding in the movement elements; it effectively breaks down Key stages 1 and 2 into sub-stages. Movement activities should give children a *breadth* of experience, focusing on the movement theme in question and drawing on the children's inventiveness as much as possible, to 'milk the theme', with frequent opportunities to reflect on the learning that is taking place. As previously indicated, movement experiences should be *differentiated* to meet a range of needs represented in any group. This requires the teacher to have knowledge of individual pupils' capabilities – their strengths and weaknesses – in order to frame tasks that challenge and encourage all pupils (Arts Council of GB, 1993). (See also chapter 7, section on 'Differentiating dance'.)

Selecting and creating

At this stage in the lesson, pupils are involved in choosing and combining material into phrases or sequences. This may be teacher- or pupil-led, depending on the maturity of the children. Children may require precise boundaries within which to create – paradoxically, inventiveness, originality in creating actually happens within *constraints*. Pupils with learning difficulties may require quite specific challenges to give focus; for example: 'your dance will have a way of moving on your hands and feet, then twizzling round, then stopping'. Supporting staff need to develop their questioning skills, in order not to hi-jack the creative process! Even a pupil who can only indicate 'yes' or 'no' is capable of making a creative decision that may have a powerful impact on the dance; for example: 'do you think we should start our dance low down, on the floor – yes or no?'. Staff would be advised to develop a *hierarchy of questioning* skills and to be able to move from open to closed questions, in order to help pupils focus and shape their ideas. For example:

- What animal shall we do our dance about?
- Will it be one that goes on land or one that lives in the water?
- Will it be an animal in the zoo or on the farm?
- Will it be a large animal or a small one?
- Will it be an elephant or a giraffe?
- Will it be an elephant – yes or no?

Leading children towards a finished piece will give credibility to their movement work. This section of the lesson, therefore, relates specifically to the Composing and Appreciating strands indicated above. Children should be encouraged to select from material that has provided the main content for the lesson, and organise their ideas into a repeatable sequence. The compositional structure and challenges set by the teacher may become increasingly complex (see chapter 5), with work appropriately differentiated to meet a range of abilities within the class (see below). Children will need to work at clarifying their ideas through practising (rehearsing) and perfecting their dance, in order to communicate their intention to an audience. Much will be gained from children sharing their work 'in progress', with peers offering constructive pointers on how they may develop it. In reflecting on their 'work in progress', they will need to consider:

- the original idea to be communicated through the dance
- movement phrases they have selected
- the structure of the dance (AB, ABA, ABACA, etc – see Chapter 5)
- starting and finishing positions
- the development of the dance – a possible climax
- introducing variety – contrasts in levels, directions, speed, energy, pathways in space, patterns, relationships between the dancers
- rhythm – use of music or accompaniment

Children should become familiar from an early age with presenting their work to others and reflecting upon and evaluating its effectiveness. Even teacher-led dance with pupils working towards or within Key stage 1 may be performed in two groups so that half the class has a chance to observe the other. Children need to develop 'active watching' (see below) and be guided in what to look for, and in describing and analysing what they have seen (Arts Council of GB, 1993). Children may need specific pointers to watch for, in order to develop their observation and interpretation skills (e.g. 'I shall ask you in a moment if you can show me what shapes the dancers made with their bodies'). In questioning pupils about dance they have seen:

> ...reference can be made to the context, content and execution of the dance. Distinction should be made between objective evaluation (what is happening, how is it happening) and subjective evaluation (how do I feel about it) (Arts Council of GB, 1993, p. 7).

Developing 'active watching'

Children need to develop their knowledge and understanding of how dance may be used as a means of communication, and to develop their aesthetic sensitivity. Their responses to dance they have watched need to be probed, to help children to realise *why* they think or react in a particular way. Children do not have to like a particular dance – indeed, dance is sometimes intended to be provocative, to shock or to disturb. Nevertheless, they should be encouraged to substantiate their opinions and to develop an appropriate dance vocabulary. Watching dance performances can be a valuable stimulus for developing ideas in children's own work and for raising awareness of performance quality. Describing and analysing dance may prompt suggestions how their own dance may be composed, performed and appreciated.

The intention behind watching professional dance is not to deskill children (or staff!) or to shatter their confidence by implying that they will never be able to achieve such technical and artistic powers of expression! Rather, ideas may be harnessed that will inform and inspire children's own work. Be sensitive to children's concentration span: sitting through a formal performance at the theatre may be too challenging for some children, especially given the social pressures and expectations of behaviour that tend to accompany the formality of many such occasions. Many dance companies now offer workshops for schools, with excellent education programmes – it may be possible for the dancers to come to the school. If not, then consider collecting examples of different kinds of dance on video – some are commercially available; alternatively, tape short extracts from TV.

Live dance may offer the heightened immediacy and power of dancers' ability to communicate, with a tremendous sense of occasion and a bringing together of different art forms (music, dance, design and technology). However, dance on video is also valuable, especially the use of close-up for highlighting facial expression and use of gesture. Dance on video also has the advantage that it can be repeated and stopped to freeze a significant moment. It can be difficult to capture the transient nature of dance otherwise. This makes it a particularly valuable teaching tool with children with learning difficulties who, to varying degrees, often struggle with recall.

In questioning children about dance they have watched, it is possible to target specific aspects. The following examples could guide children's responses not only to a piece of professional dance but also in evaluating (appreciating) work of their peers. Some of the questions will need adapting according to children's age, ability and understanding. For example (based on Siddall, 1985):

- *the whole dance:*
  - was it easy to follow? did it tell a story?
  - was it interesting, or were there parts that were less interesting?
  - was it clear?
  - were there any unusual parts that surprised you and made you take notice?
  - did the dance and the accompaniment go well together?

- *the dance idea:*
  - could you understand what the dancers were wanting to tell us?
  - how could you tell from the movements?
  - how did the dancers feel about the idea they wanted to tell us?
  - did you learn something new about that idea from watching the dance?
  - was the idea relevant to your own experience?

- *the movement content:*
  - were the movements 'right' for the dance?
  - were the movements varied enough to keep your interest?
  - how did the dancers use the space? was it effective?
  - were the movements symbolic (about something) or were they expressing a feeling? how could you tell?

- *actions:*
  - what actions do you particularly remember?
  - were the actions interesting? why?
  - were they based on actions in real life?
  - did the actions relate to one another and flow easily?
  - did the dancers maintain their stance?

- *use of space:*
  - how were the dancers arranged?
  - did they use the whole space, or just part of it?
  - did the dancers make shapes, lines or patterns? how?
  - did the use of space help tell us about the dance idea?

- *dynamics:*
  - was the dance varied?
  - which bits did you find effective? why?
  - how was the dance made interesting?
  - were there bits of the dance that were very different, contrasted?

- *relationships:*
  - how many dancers were there? one? two? three? lots?
  - was there a clear relationship between the dancers?
  - could you see all the dancers or were some hidden from view (masked)?
  - how did the dancers perform: all at the same time (unison), in canon (one after the other)?
  - were some dancers still whilst the others moved (solo? duets? small groups?)

- could you tell how the dancers felt about one another? did they like one another in the dance?
- did the way they moved in relation to one another help us understand? (e.g. away from one another, towards one another, around one another, some down low, some up high, etc.)

● *structure:*
- were there parts of the dance that were repeated (the same)?
- were the contrasts effective?
- did the idea of the dance become clear?
- were the sections of the dance too short, too long or the right length?
- was the ending effective? did it seem right to you?

● *performance:*
- were the dancers sincere and fully involved?
- did they fully extend their movements?
- did they project and communicate throughout?
- did they sustain the style of the dance throughout?

● *accompaniment:*
- was the music appropriate for the dance idea (and vice versa)?
- did the movements match the phrases in the music?
- (if the dancers used objects) did the objects help add to the dance?
- were the costumes (if used) effective? *or* what costumes or props would go well with the dance?
- did the set contribute to the dance? *or* what scenery would go well with the dance?
- how did/could lighting help the dance?
- how important is the title of the dance? *or* what title would you give this dance?

● *overall impression:*
- did you like the dance? why/why not? (Beware group dynamics: encourage children to comment constructively, rather than offer unsubstantiated criticism)
- how did it make you feel?
- were there bits you feel could be improved? how?
- how was the dance affecting the rest of the audience?
- did everyone react the same way or did people react differently?
- did you feel the same throughout the dance or did your feelings change?

Dance styles and traditions

Children need to develop their *skills* in dance, but also their *knowledge and understanding* of dance. All dance consists of a relationship between intention, action, space, dynamics, design, music, dancers and audience. These components are shaped, structured and given form; the way in which they are combined will determine the particular dance style. Certain genres of dance are recognisable by characterising features; for example, much African dance is low-slung (bent knees) with wide gait and the back curved forwards or backwards. However, within each genre there may be many variations – the dance of Africa being a case in point. Children may be introduced to the way different dance styles exploit pattern, rhythm, line and form. Experiencing dance from a range of historical and cultural contexts will offer children important access to their heritage. The Arts Council of GB (1993) makes the point that:

> All dances have a cultural context and reflect something about the society and times in which they were created. Understanding the cultural context is part of understanding dance (para 2.12, p.6).

The Arts Council of GB (1993) also indicates how dance can offer the benefit of an 'inside-out' approach:

> Through composing dances pupils become familiar with the language of dance from the inside, and understand how it can enrich their lives and those of others. They are enabled to 'read' and to discuss dance works, and so gain access to an important field of human expression (para 2.11, p 6).

The implication is that experiencing dance from different styles and traditions should not be seen merely as enrichment or an 'add on' to the curriculum. Rather, that so much more may be gained by seeing world dance as an integral aspect of dance education: to inspire and inform children's own work. (The appendix of lesson plans contains examples of work developed from particular dance styles and traditions.) It is crucial that an appropriate point of contact is offered so that the dance has relevance to the child's own experience and ability. It is important to be selective: narrow the focus over which parts of the dance the children are to explore. Opportunity should be found for children to gain something of the technical skill involved, but also to bring their own creativity and inventiveness, to make it 'their own'. There are several ways in which this may be achieved.

Lifting an idea embodied in a dance

Children may be asked to interpret the narrative content of a dance before harnessing the idea to create their own dance on the same theme. For example, after the children have watched an extract of ballet on video they may be asked:

• Consider one of the characters: was there a particular gesture or action he or she performed more than once? Copy that action, then add another one, then make up a new one (in character). Perform the sequence over again until fluent.

• What was a particular dancer feeling at a certain moment? (happy? sad? angry?) What actions did he or she perform which told us that? Choose two to copy and practise, then add a new one (in character). Perform the sequence over again until fluent.

Working with a step pattern creatively

Children may be taught a specific sequence of steps then asked to use the pattern to choreograph an original routine. They may be required to design pathways and consider how they will perform the step pattern in relation to the other dancers in their group. They may be asked to teach their routine to others! The 'ladder approach' (Lewis, 1991) is helpful in enabling children to self-differentiate: finding their own level, so that they are aware of the new challenge but have the option of reverting to the 'rung' below. This is useful, as children can always be reminded of this, and not worry about 'failing' or letting down the group if they (literally!) can't keep pace. I have taught the example below to fully integrated groups of able-bodied and disabled children; the 'pushers' of those children in wheelchairs performed the steps on their behalf whilst those in wheelchairs performed appropriate arm actions! Let's see just how complex we could make the 'grapevine' step (Zorba the Greek), which is a repeated step pattern, involving crossing one foot in front then behind the other to travel sideways:

• moving sideways on cue (when the music starts – associating sound with movement)
• step–close (small step sideways, bringing the other foot to close feet together)
• step–close, to include a change of direction
• step–close, to include a change of direction and performed faster
• step–in front (step to the left, right foot to cross in front)

- step–in front, to include a change of direction
- step–in front, to include a change of direction and performed faster
- step–behind (step to the left, right foot to cross behind)
- step–behind, to include a change of direction
- step–behind, to include a change of direction and performed faster
- step–in front, and step–behind, combining the above
- step–in front, and step–behind, combining the above, with a change of direction
- step–in front, and step–behind, combining the above, with a change of direction and performed faster
- performing the step as a skip
- tracing pathways as a whole group (e.g. spiral shapes, maintaining the line)
- performing in lines, facing one another
- choreographing a routine, to include changes of arm shapes (hands on hips, above head, on shoulders, touching shoulders of others, etc.)

Using steps from a dance style to devise original routines.

Children may be taught a range of steps from a particular dance style, with gradual introduction of steps that are more challenging. Children may learn how some of the steps reflect the context in which they evolved; for example, the 'break for freedom' step in Lindy Hop (see below), a version of North American Jazz, which derived from Black dance of exiled African slaves, influenced by Western music. Lindy Hop involves low slung posture, swivelly hips and transferring weight from one foot to another. It may be helpful to analyse the challenges involved in certain steps, so that increasingly complex steps may be introduced when children are ready, with tasks appropriately differentiated. For example:

Transferring weight
- 'side-step' (step to the side, then close other foot to bring feet together; arms bent at the elbow and forearms raised, like Thunderbird puppets)
- 'tap-step' (tap floor with toe of shoe to the front, then bring back to close feet together; swap to other foot; arms bent, swing casually forwards and backwards, fingers pointing down)
- 'kick-step' (kick across the body, flinging foot; swap to other foot; arms extended, bent casually at the elbow)
- 'swing-step' (hand on hip, the other hand as if carrying a tray above the head, feet swivel from side to side)

- 'Shorty George' (shuffling feet, with shoulders slouched, arms dangling with index fingers pointing at shoes)

Transferring weight, including a jump
- 'chassee' (as 'side-step', but performed as a sideways gallop, changing direction)
- 'break for freedom' ('kick-step', but with a jump, also alternating a fling of the arms and change direction)
- 'boogie back' (clap hands, then small jump backwards, landing on one foot slightly before the other, with a swing of the hips)

Gesture – holding stillness for a specified number of counts
- 'frog' (jump into a pose with bent knees and extended arms)
- 'scarecrow' (jump into a pose with knees together, arms bent, head dangling and a daft expression!)
- 'photo' (jump into a pose as if caught on camera by surprise)
- 'rock the baby' (exaggerated cradling action, raising elbows and rocking)
- 'gaze afar' (exaggerated looking to four counts, hand shielding eyes, other hand on hip, following through 180 degrees; preceeded by four small trots)

There is a range of ways in which children may be extended further:
- performing steps on the spot, keeping within an eight-beat cycle
- introducing changes of direction (sideways, forwards and backwards)
- performing steps 'round the clock' (i.e. quarter turns, keeping in rhythm)
- introducing those steps that include a jump and/or a turn
- performing them fast (to 'boogie woogie' as opposed to 'swing' musical accompaniment)
- introducing arm actions (concentrate on children getting the feet right first, before worrying about arms as well!)
- including steps that demand holding stillness for a specified number of counts
- inventing a new step (e.g. 'the chewing gum on the shoe step', 'the chicken', etc.)
- combining steps in sequence:
  - follow-my-leader (teacher-led dance, changing steps)
  - copy-cat dance (take turns to follow partner's lead)
  - sequence three actions with a partner: one chosen by each, and the third negotiated

- sequence a routine with specific challenges: e.g. that includes a change of direction, a step that has a jump with it, a section where both partners perform a different step, a step where both partners are still, etc.

A dance module

It will be apparent from this chapter how even a seemingly unpromising 'idea for dance' may be 'unpacked', to give in-depth experience based on related movement themes. This may lead to an extended programme of work, developed over a half term. It will be important over time to offer children breadth and balance in exploration of the movement elements, and in intoducing children to a range of dance styles and traditions to inspire and inform their own work. Additionally, the teacher will need to cater for the range of individual needs within the group and children's natural 'starting points' for dance (see chapter 2). The following chapter will address these issues in greater depth.

There follows here an example of a possible dance module over a half term, with planning for progression and continuity both within and between sessions. It illustrates how children may be gradually led to explore a particular dance style, with opportunities for consolidation and improvement as well as learning increasingly complex steps. It also indicates how some of the approaches described in the previous section may translate in practice! The module addresses progression in children's ability to *perform*, *compose* and *appraise* dance. Assessment opportunities need to be planned within each lesson so that all pupils are monitored over the module. It is geared at a group of pupils with moderate learning difficulties, working within Key stage 2. However, I have taught the module successfully to youngsters with severe learning difficulties, concentrating especially on lessons one to three, repeating each one, to make a six-session module.

It is possible to differentiate the content of each lesson thus:
- modification
  - partnering a supporting adult or more able peer;
  - concentrating on improving simpler steps (transferring weight, rather than more complex steps with jumps that involve turns in time with the music);
  - concentrating on steps rather than arm actions (or vice versa);
  - dancing to slower music, e.g. 'Swing' rather than 'Boogie Woogie'

- extension
  - partnering a peer, or supporting ('teaching') a less able peer
  - refining complex steps including jumps and turns, keeping in rhythm
  - performing steps with poise and fluency
  - combining arm actions with steps
  - holding stillness for specified beats (counting inside head)
  - maintaining correct posture (e.g. low stance of dance for Jazz)

Example: 'North American Jazz' (Lindy Hop)

Group: Key stage 2

Objectives: sequencing dance forms (Programme of Study ref. 3b)
composing and controlling their movements (Programme of Study ref. 3a)

Assessment criteria:
- ability to fit dance steps to rhythmic accompaniment
- ability to maintain body shapes and posture in dance forms
- ability to perform dance steps of varying complexity
- ability to perform dance steps with regard to others
- ability to select steps and give shape to devise a repeatable sequence
- ability to comment on the performance of others, describing what they did and how

	Warm-up exercises	Development and exploration	Selecting and creating
Week 1: Transferring weight	<ul><li>Sitting on floor: rock side to side, transferring weight to alternate hands</li><li>Standing: rock side to side, onto one foot then the other</li><li>Stretching up high, curling slowly down low</li><li>Shaking out hands from high to low</li><li>Shaking each foot in turn to front, side, back</li><li>Stand on one leg: tap floor with toes, alternating as quickly as possible</li><li>Bend knees, legs apart, draw circle with bottom</li></ul>	<ul><li>Posture: low slung, wide gait, bottom sticking out, bending forwards, relaxed dangling arms</li><li>Follow-me steps to 'Swing' music: 'side-step' 'tap step' 'kick step' 'swing step' 'frog'</li><li>Practise each step, concentrating on feet; extension task to think about arms</li><li>Try walking round the room, performing certain steps</li></ul>	<ul><li>Whole class improvised dance, led by teacher</li><li>Children to recall some of the steps and their names</li></ul>
Week 2: Transferring weight in time	<ul><li>As before, doing each exercise to count of eight beats</li></ul>	<ul><li>Revise steps from last week</li><li>Introduce changes of direction, forwards and backwards – to count of eight</li><li>New steps: 'scarecrow' 'photo' 'Shorty George'</li><li>Practise steps with a partner</li></ul>	<ul><li>Improvised 'copy cat' dance in pairs, taking it in turns to be the leader</li><li>Including advancing and retreating</li><li>Agreeing finishing position ('frog', 'photo' or 'scarecrow')</li><li>Half class watch at a time, commenting on those keeping time with music and one another</li></ul>

Week			
Week 3: Transferring weight, with a jump	As before • Bobbing heels off ground to eight counts • Jumping on spot to eight counts (*keep* jumps & steps small) • Trotting for eight counts • Eight ski-swings of arms, stretching up on eighth • Curling up for eight • Repeat sequence	• 'Follow me' revision of steps so far • Introduce new steps, involving a jump: 'break for freedom' 'chassee' 'boogie back' • Practise steps with a partner	• Partner dance: each to choose a step, then agree a third step • Practise the three steps in sequence, repeating • Include advancing and retreating from one another; also one step that involves a jump • Half the class perform at a time; children to watch a specific pair, and be ready to describe choice of steps
Week 4: Transferring weight with a jump and a turn	As before • Include jumping 'round the clock' – quarter turn jumps	• 'Follow me' revision of steps so far • Practise certain steps 'round the clock': 'tap-step' 'kick-step' • Teach new steps: 'rock-the-baby' 'gaze afar'	• Partner dance: three steps in sequence, repeating • Include one step 'round the clock', one step that involves a jump, and one where they advance and retreat to eight counts • Half the class perform at a time, endeavouring to keep time with the music • Audience to comment as last week
Week 5: Gesture holding stillness	As before • Include holding stillness for eight counts	• 'Follow me' revision of steps so far • Children to invent new step, practise in pairs; give step a name! • Teach new step to everyone, precise arm and foot movements;	• Partner dance: four steps in repeated sequence • Include one step 'round the clock', a jump travelling, and a gesture held for eight counts • One step must be one of the newly invented! • Half the class perform at a time, endeavouring to keep time with the music, and to make transitions smooth • Audience to comment as last week
Week 6: Refining	As before	• Follow-me revision of dance steps • Categorising steps: travelling, jumping, turning, gesture • Emphasising poise and posture in execution of steps • In pairs, practise a range of steps, offering one another advice on how to improve • Fit dance steps to 'Swing', then faster 'Boogie Woogie'	• Whole class dance, negotiating a routine to be repeated • Practise routine in pairs (label A and B) • Half the class perform at a time; at the end of each sequence, Bs have eight counts to find new A, travelling with 'swing step' (As perform 'swing step' on the spot) • Audience to comment on individual flair!

CHAPTER 7

Developing Quality Teaching in Dance

This chapter aims to sharpen the teacher's ability to ensure progression and continuity in dance. It examines the role of the teacher and explores certain strategies for teaching dance. It probes assumptions over 'progression in dance', and considers related issues of assessment and differentiation to meet the full range of needs within a class. Further sections are aimed to support the teacher in 'reading' the class: evaluating the lesson in progress and afterwards, and suggestions for 'troubleshooting' difficulties that may arise.

The role of the teacher

As with other areas of the curriculum, the teacher of dance faces the basic challenges of ensuring each individual pupil has access to the curriculum and is enabled to learn; secondly, that pupils are motivated to learn through careful class management. Strategies for adapting teaching and learning to meet individual needs are considered in a later section to this chapter, entitled 'Differentiating dance work'. This section and the following one will focus on the second challenge identified above: to create effective learning opportunities that will be intrinsically motivating and help keep pupils 'on task'.

From reading previous chapters it will be clear by now that effective dance teaching requires teachers to have a clear notion of what children are expected to learn: knowledge, skills and understanding of a particular aspect of dance. Teachers will find greater confidence and security from having a clear conception of development in dance. This is not to imply that dance teaching becomes heavily directive – the opposite, in fact. Paradoxically, secure grasp of benchmarks of development may *liberate* teachers towards adopting more flexible strategies for extending pupils and guiding them towards new levels (refer to the spiral curriculum model in chapter 3). Teachers' own understanding will enable them to be more responsive to pupils' initiatives and to seize and build on cues from the pupils.

Dance teaching exemplifies principles of active learning – pupils engaged in modifying information they receive rather than being 'drip-fed'. Chapter 1 considered the value of active learning long-term in fostering pupils' sense of autonomy and resourcefulness as well as facilitating recall of exciting, memorable learning experiences involving high energy levels. Outcomes in dance need not be predetermined but should allow for individuality, with pupils appropriately challenged in tasks which enable them to take greater responsibility and control of the learning process. An underlying premise is that children are more likely to be motivated and care about work over which they perceive themselves to have ownership.

While for the teacher this may be a useful management device for preventing disaffection, for the pupils this interactive approach (Collis and Lacey, 1996) represents an important, empowering way to learn (as described in chapter 1). This will arise through genuine respect for the pupils' contributions, which are valued and positively developed by the teacher. This does not conflict with the notion of the teacher planning a structured lesson: rather, the structure is *covert*, and to the pupils appears as boundaries within which to make creative choices and decisions. For the teacher, this involves setting tasks for pupils in which they may find success but not too easily. Ultimately, the aim is for pupils to succeed without help from teacher (or peers), and to be able to transfer and generalise learning to other situations.

The amount of support and help has to be just the right amount for each pupil. Staff should aim to fade out the amount of prompting: whether physically supporting a pupil (with respect for cultural sensitivities), gesturing or demonstrating an action for the pupil to imitate, verbally reminding a pupil, or being there as 'back up' while the pupil performs a task independently. Essentially, staff should be (literally!) 'one step behind' in the assistance they offer: allowing pupils to experiment and attempt a task before intervening and sensitively providing the kind of support required to enable the child to succeed. Prompting in this way may be considered as a 'scaffold' (Wood *et al*, 1976) between a pupil's present level of attainment and a future achievable level.

Vygotsky (1978) describes this as the 'zone of proximal development' the gap between a child's present level of development and the potential level of development that is bridged when the teacher enables the pupil to achieve beyond his or her previous capacity. A route through may be provided by harnessing principles of a three-stage 'planning–doing–reviewing' process, advocated by proponents of the High/Scope Curriculum founded in 1961, by Weikart, then Director of Special Education in Michigan, USA:

1. *Planning*: staff discuss and help shape a child's intention (whether an action or skill to be performed, a movement sequence to be executed, or a dance to be choreographed)
2. *Doing*: staff then enable the child to achieve his or her goal through supporting sensitively in the way described above
3. *Reviewing*: staff then reflect with the child on his or her attainment, with a view towards negotiating future learning, based on the child's wishes and his or her learning need as perceived by the teacher.

Of central importance is the idea that children learn most effectively when the educational experiences provided are in tune with each child's level of development, are initiated by the child himself and enable the child to reflect his own interests (Mitchell, pp. 67-8).

Teaching strategies for dance

Gough (1993) highlights the importance of even an inexperienced teacher of dance appearing confident and actively involved. This requires a sensitive balance (acquired with experience) between demonstrating and joining in, and observing and unobtrusively recognising when certain pupils may need physical or verbal participation by the teacher, suggesting ideas or helping to solve problems. Gough indicates the importance of using appropriate language and limiting the amount of information to be processed; also of using the voice expressively to challenge and inspire movement quality, to set phrasing and establish rhythm:

Stretch, come on even further... S – T – R – E – T – C – H!
Travel 2..3.., travel 2..3.., TURN.., and hold (Gough, 1993, p. 35).

Gough identifies several strategies for the teacher of dance; the following pointers develop some of her ideas.

Demonstration (of a task, a skill, or set material to be acquired)

• It is preferable to present a complete sequence to give pupils an overall intention of what is to be aimed for, with commentary to point up significant features and to give a sense of continuity and flow

- Question the pupils about what they saw to assist them in recognising and describing observed movement and translating it into their own body
- Some pupils may not be able to tell or even show you what you did, but they may be able to show you what you did *not* do; for example, ask the pupils 'did I travel round the room this way....or was it like this?'
- Break down material into manageable sections that concentrate on a particular aspect to be perfected
- Allow sufficient time for pupils to repeat and clarify a section before gradually accumulating
- This approach risks becoming over-directive; rather than always being presented by the teacher, tasks may be *pupil-led* (e.g. a warm-up exercise)
- Ideas may be based on a *pupil's initiative*: the teacher developing a cue from a pupil, or the pupil teaching imaginative material to the rest of the class
- Consider whether a task may be presented as an *idea* to be extended or embellished, not necessarily copied directly
- Copying directly may be important for certain pupils in raising awareness of new possibilities; they may then feel suitably inspired or informed to develop the original idea into a new movement
- Consider presenting a task as a *challenge* for certain pupils, to encourage greater effort, or clarity and precision; for example, 'do you think you can remember to keep your knees bent and your body low as you travel round?'

Problem-solving (*a creative response by pupils to challenges set by the teacher*)

- Pupils are invited to discover and produce options based on the material (e.g. 'how many different ways to bounce can you find?'; 'can you make the links between your actions really smooth?'; 'include one moment in your dance where both of you dance side by side'; 'make sure you have a clear starting position and finishing position'; 'how will the audience know that your dance is about someone who is sad?' etc.)
- Tasks are necessarily open-ended and designed to produce a range of outcomes; individuals may need to be challenged as they work, to ensure they are suitably extending themselves

- A range of achievements may be celebrated, with praise given for effort, degree of engagement, concentration, not just progress beyond previous attainment (see following section on 'Progression in Dance')
- An appropriate ethos needs to be fostered where pupils may feel confident in their expression, without fear of failure or ridicule

Self-evaluation (pupils work at a task for a set period of time)

- This requires pupils to break down the work into sections, to be aware of problems, to repeat and refine their work (a movement exercise, a section of a set dance, a piece of choreography)
- Clearly, working in this way demands a level of competence and movement memory, concentration and sense of personal responsibility, although pupils may be enabled to work in this way through judicious partnering with a more able peer or supporting member of staff (akin to the 'planning–doing–reviewing' process, described above)
- The teacher may support pupils through demonstrating aspects of the task (see above), either to individuals or pairs or else to the whole group
- Consider sharing work in progress so that pupils have the opportunity to support one another in offering constructive suggestions, and which will effectively enable tasks to be broken down into more manageable sections

Collaboration (co-operation and negotiation in learning, rather than competition or rivalry)

- Opportunities should be created for everyone to contribute, no matter how 'small' the idea; this may be a legitimated choice between (for example) deciding everyone should practise jumping on one leg or two, not just larger decisions in developing group dances
- It is the teacher's responsibility to ensure pupils are enabled to offer a creative initiative, by questioning and challenging appropriately; even 'closed' questions may be potentially empowering: e.g. 'Karen, shall we go backwards now instead of forwards – yes or no?'
- The teacher needs to foster an expectation of tolerance and a willingness to share and learn from one another; pupils may be challenged to negotiate and organise their work in respect of one

another: size of groupings, group dynamics and strategic placing of
supporting staff may facilitate conditions conducive to collaborative
working
• Making choices requires pupils to have a knowledge-base from which
  to make an informed selection: the memory span of certain pupils
  needs to be considered, as this will have a bearing on their ability to
  offer a creative suggestion and when this may be timed within the
  lesson
• Tasks need to be clearly structured with a distinct focus as this will
  enable pupils to make an appropriate creative suggestion within
  defined bounds or constraints
• The teacher may provide clear parameters which will inherently
  ensure that pupils in a group are required to collaborate; for example,
  insist on one favourite action or idea from each person, then an extra
  one about which they all have to agree.

Progression in dance

What do we mean by 'progress in dance'? I have raised the same question
elsewhere in relation to the other arts (Peter, 1994, 1995, 1996a and b, Wills
and Peter, 1996). Is 'progress' being able to do things that are more
challenging?...Or the same thing but 'better'?...Or the same thing but with
more confidence and understanding?... It can – and should – be all of these,
of course. It is worth referring back to the spiral curriculum model in
chapter 3, whereby progression will involve circling back to re-visit an
activity with increasing complexity. The Arts Council of GB (1993)
recognises progression as the extent to which pupils are able to *compose*,
perform and *appreciate* dance with increasing understanding, complexity,
control, depth and independence. Characteristically, some pupils with SEN
may have patchy profiles relating to these aspects. For example, pupils with
motor disability may develop acute understanding of dance while being
more limited in increasing their physical skills. It is worth re-stating here
the importance of enabling pupils to work to their strengths (e.g. as
choreographer, director, critic, audience) as well as improving areas of
relative weakness.

The Arts Council of GB (1993) usefully summarises pointers relating to
progression in dance, which may be considered as basic criteria on which to
gauge development. The section on assessing achievement later in this
chapter offers more specific guidelines.

4.14 Pupils generally progress from:
- using given criteria to using their own criteria to evaluate performance
- simple tasks to more complex ones
- natural movements to more deliberate and complex performance.

Progression is also cyclical and pupils generally move between:
- dependence and independence in learning
- performing given tasks to being able to structure their own work as their capacity to deal with more complex tasks develops.

4.15 Progression in dance can be seen in:
- range of type of movement and use of parts of the body
- appropriate use of energy, flow and bodily tension
- physical ability and confidence
- clarity of shape, line and form
- efficiency and fluency in movement
- developing specific dance vocabulary
- range of response to rhythm
- increasing complexity in use of rhythm
- linking of the familiar and unfamiliar
- ability to move from the literal to the abstract
- ability to move from given tasks to choosing own task and finding own resource material
- ability to move from describing to comparing, analysing, evaluating
- ability to identify and record intention and outcome.

Differentiating dance work

Differentiation is a process of matching teaching content to individual needs, with the intention of promoting equality of access. Differentiation is not just a principle of teaching aimed at those with SEN: it should apply to the overall task for the lesson and to individual tasks within the lesson (Arts Council of GB, 1993). Most children in mainstream as well as special education may experience a mis-match in their potential achievement in dance around adolescence, quite apart from the additional difficulties affecting those with SEN. Changes in body weight, proportion and shape, as well as emotional and social changes, may prompt a temporary regression and sluggishness. Fortunately, in more recent times, dance has become fairly 'cool' amongst the teenage sub-culture!

It is probably true to say that dance teaching has tended to rely over-heavily on setting tasks that can be interpreted in different ways ('differentiation by outcome'). Arguably, however, many children with learning disabilities in particular may have a relatively limited creative sense of resourcefulness and inventiveness, in pushing themselves beyond the familiar, even if capable of such achievement. Dance work can be much more specifically focused to address individual needs (for example, through 'differentiation by task', where a number of different activities may be set to cater for a range of abilities within the group). However, there are a number of other differentiation strategies also at the teacher's disposal (based on Barthorpe, 1992):

- *The 'wallet" idea:* resources/items with inherent, developmentally appropriate challenges for pupils of all abilities.
Example: tapes with extracts of music, with a range of rhythmic patterns
  - some arhythmic/amorphous/atmospheric (e.g. synthesized, electronic music)
  - some in simple rhythmic patterns (e.g. march, waltz, etc)
  - some in compound metre (skipping rhythms, e.g. the nursery rhyme 'Girls and Boys come out to Play')
  - some that are syncopated (e.g. reggae, calypso, samba, etc.)
  - some with denser textures (e.g. African ceremonial music)

- *The 'jigsaw' approach*: allocating specific tasks to challenge pupils according to their respective abilities, which may then be combined to create a group piece.
Example: a class 'Rainforest' dance composition involving:
  - some maintaining an action in unison, keeping with the pulse of the music accompaniment (e.g. growing and shrinking, and swaying as a group 'plant')
  - some performing two contrasting actions in unison, listening for a change in the music accompaniment (e.g. pairs growing into a 'plant' shape together, holding stillness, then falling and rolling when 'felled')
  - some matching changes of actions, moving in relation to one another (e.g. groups of 'animals' sequencing three movements, representative of the chosen creature, moving amongst the plants)
  - some performing solo/partner dances, involving more complex/combined actions (e.g. 'lumberjacks' sequencing actions representative of typical tasks, performed in relation to others about their work)

• *The 'layered' approach* : differing challenges presented to extend pupils according to their ability.

Example: performing the 'grapevine' step (in Zorba's Dance):
 - some to achieve step–close (taking a small sideways step, then bringing the other foot together)
 - some to achieve step–in front (as above, but crossing one foot in front of the other)
 - some to achieve step–behind (as above, but crossing one foot behind the other)
 - some to achieve step–in front, step–behind (combining all the above)

• *Differentiation by task*: several points of entry into the same activity where the pupils create within the parameters defined by the teacher.

Example: watching an extract on video of a 'pas de deux' from a ballet:
 - some to indicate their reaction through spontaneous responses (positive: smiling? negative: flinching or crying?)
 - some to comment on who was dancing (men? women? how many? etc.), and what they did, and to name (or show) some of the actions (jumping, skipping, arm movements, etc.)
 - some to comment on how the dancers performed their actions (both at the same time? one after the other? in the same place? up high/down low? etc.)
 - some to comment on the narrative/story-line (did they like each other? why do you think that? how could you tell? were there parts you thought could have been performed differently? etc.)

• *Differentiation by outcome*: the same activity delivered with varying responses according to pupils' respective ability.

Example: performing 'stalking' actions as a section of a whole group 'tiger dance':
 - some achieving crawling action on hands and knees, or raising arms alternately with support while travelling in their wheelchairs
 - some crawling on hands and knees, lifting their limbs and placing them slowly
 - some crawling on hands and knees in different directions, lifting and placing limbs slowly and silently
 - some crawling on hands and knees in different directions, lifting and placing limbs slowly and silently, with appropriate facial expression (eyes darting and menacing)

- *Different methods of learning style*: accessing aspects of the curriculum to different pupils.

  Example: prompt cards to support pupils choreographing sections for a dance, which may be ordered (on a felt board) as a script:
  - some with picture cues (e.g. a series of cats performing different actions)
  - some with abstract symbols (e.g. writing pattern motifs, arrows, spiral shapes, etc.)
  - some with action word vocabulary (e.g. stalk, pounce, roll)
  - some with feeling word vocabulary (e.g. hungry, determined, lazy)

- *Evaluating work*: taking account of the extent to which achievements reflect pupils' expected potential, with the efforts of all pupils valued with regard to their respective stage of development.

Assessing achievement

In order to make a judgement about children's achievements, the teacher will need a clear grasp of teaching and learning objectives for the group and individuals within the group. Assessment should be an integral part of the teaching process, essential in enabling teachers to review and plan their work and for pupils to chart their achievements. This may include periodic 'summative' reporting (e.g. to parents) but mostly will comprise continuing 'formative' assessment by which the teacher will be able to plan for children's needs. The teacher will need to develop systematic strategies for assessing children: both in regular observations and in ensuring all children receive equal consideration. Assessment should take account not just of the *product* (the dance itself) but also the *process* towards achieving the dance.

Observation will be the most appropriate means for assessing achievement in movement and dance: how pupils respond to a particular task, and whether the task needs breaking down further. Discussion – questioning pupils – may reveal their thinking and intentions and something of their knowledge and understanding of the dance process. It may also be possible to structure assessment opportunities: tasks specifically for the purposes of assessment; or targeting supporting staff (suitably briefed) to track or work with a particular pupil, with a view to monitoring his or her responses. Alternatively, a supporting member of staff may take a managing role for the class for a while, whilst the teacher works with an indivdual child or group of children. Video can also provide a useful tool for recording pupils' achievements, especially as signficant developments may happen behind the teacher's back! Supporting staff may be briefed to 'track' a particular pupil or pupils (as discreetly as possible!), although some pupils may find the presence of the camera off-putting. Replaying work recorded on video may also facilitate pupils' involement in their own self-assessment (those with learning difficulties struggle with recall to varying degrees).

The Arts Council of GB (1993) indicates the kind of evidence for pupils' attainment in dance:

• knowledge about dance
• aesthetic awareness
• ability to communicate aesthetic appreciation
• ability to make discerning judgements
• movement vocabulary
• ability to structure movement material
• imagination in ideas for making dances
• originality and integrity in using the various components of dance
• capacity to make symbolic meaning through movements
• ability to express intentions successfully through dance
• expressive power in performance (para 4.20, p. 19).

Figure 7.2 offers a proforma for recording individual achievement in dance. A pupil's progress over six separate occasions may be monitored; for example, once a week over a half-term, or once every half-term over a school year. Teacher's comments will be crucial in order to indicate the basis (the evidence) on which pupils' responses have been assessed; also to indicate future learning needs. A grading system of 1 to 4 is suggested (see Figure 7.1), to indicate achievement within the sub-stages identified in chapter 2 (summarised more fully in figure 5.1):

• 1 for achievement within the 'Emergent' phase
• 2 for achievement within the 'Expressive' phase
• 3 for achievement within the 'Impressive' phase
• 4 for achievement within the 'Communicative' phase

This is a fairly crude profile but will give some indication of pupils' attainment according to their understanding and use of the elements of dance. There are also additional categories on the proforma for commenting on pupils' developing understanding of dance. This too may be drastically summarised across the four stages on the recording proforma (see figure 7.1; refer to figure 5.1 for fuller details).

Evaluating the lesson

So was it any good? It is one thing to have a good idea for how the lesson should develop, but it is another thing to realise this by guiding and

EMERGENT (Pre/lower KS1)	EXPRESSIVE (Upper KS1)	IMPRESSIVE (Lower KS2)	COMMUNICATIVE (Upper KS2/3)
Body awareness: 1 body parts	2 transferring weight	3 leading actions	4 posture and body shape
Actions: 1 basic actions (go, stop, jump, turn)	2 basic actions with greater control	3 complex/ subtle actions (gesture)	4 smooth transitions and flexibility in movement
Space: 1 directions (forwards, backwards, sideways)	2 levels (high/mid/low)	3 uses personal and general space	4 designs pathways
Dynamics: 1 uses contrasts in speed (fast/slow)	2 uses direct/flexible movement	3 uses free/bound movement	4 uses tension – firm/fine movement
Relationships: 1 accepts support, trusts to another	2 balances weight with another	3 exerts force against another (push, pull, lift, lower, support)	4 harnesses ideas of harmony/opposition
Appreciation: 1 basic vocabulary, feeling responses	2 recalling what happened	3 describing what happened and how it was put together	4 describing and interpreting a dance
Composition: 1 teacher-led improvisation	2 ordering actions into a sequence	3 simple solo/partner dance	4 more complex group dance

Figure 7.1: Profile for achievement in dance

supporting pupils effectively. The first section offers some pointers by which to 'read' what is happening in the class (based on Siddall, 1985). The second section offers guidance on evaluating the effectiveness of the lesson afterwards (based on Wills and Peter, 1996).

During the lesson

The pupils in the space

- What have they been doing before the dance lesson?
- What mood are they in as they enter the dance space, and how might this affect their attitude to the class?
- Should the warm-up energise them, or calm them and focus their attention?
- Does each individual have sufficient space to be able to move without bumping their neighbour?
- Are the children aware of one another, able to travel around the room without bumping or bunching?
- Do the children use the space fully?

INDIVIDUAL PROGRESS IN DANCE

Name ....

Class ....

1 → 4

began → acquired

	Date Comments, Observations, Future Priorities	Date Comments, Observations, Future Priorities	Date Comments, Observations, Future Priorities
Ability to use ACTIONS with control: travel, jump, turn, balance, gesture, stop			
Ability to use the BODY with awareness: shape, size, selective use of body parts			
Ability to use SPACE: personal and general space, directions, levels, pathways			
Ability to use DYNAMICS: fast/slow, direct/flexible, strong/light, free/bound			
Ability to use RELATIONSHIPS: proximity, sequence, spatial relationships, supporting ('receiving', 'shared', 'controlling')			
Ability to APPRECIATE dance: understanding and interpreting movement			
Ability to COMPOSE dance: sequence movements for meaning			

	Date Comments, Observations, Future Priorities	Date Comments, Observations, Future Priorities	Date Comments, Observations, Future Priorities
Ability to use ACTIONS with control: travel, jump, turn, balance, gesture, stop			
Ability to use the BODY with awareness: shape, size, selective use of body parts			
Ability to use SPACE: personal and general space, directions, levels, pathways			
Ability to use DYNAMICS: fast/slow, direct/flexible, strong/light, bound/free			
Ability to use RELATIONSHIPS: proximity, sequence, spatial relationships, supporting ('receiving', 'shared', 'controlling')			
Ability to APPRECIATE dance: understanding and interpreting movement			
Ability to COMPOSE dance: sequence movement for meaning			

Figure 7.2: Recording sheet for individual progress in dance

Body

- Do the movements flow into one another easily, fluently and with flexibility?
- Can you see an awkward, fumbly change? Could you or one of the children suggest a way to resolve it?
- Is each part of the movement fully extended, clear, precise and executed with concentration and intent?
- Does the sequence have a shape, does it form a phrase?
- Do they maintain posture or particular stance?

Actions

- Does everyone understand the task?
- Could it be broken down, to be made more specific?
- If one person has understood the task well, could they be asked to demonstrate? (their control, poise, elevation?)
- Has someone come up with a particularly good idea that they could demonstrate? Could a specific point be made from it?
- Does a quirky response suggest a new idea to you?
- Would it be helpful to turn the task upside down and ask them to do the *opposite* of the original task?
- Could certain pupils be challenged to incorporate a jump or turn?

Space

- Is the class making the best use of the available space or are they bunching?
- Do they understand the reason for using the space well?
- Would it help to ask them to bunch together, then find a space a long way from everyone else?
- Would suggesting images help, e.g. 'wriggling like a wiggly worm'
- Is the class making use of various directions?
- Are they clear about directions?
- Could you suggest changes of direction?
- Could you suggest a specific pathway?

Levels

- Does everyone seem to be working on the same level?
- Could you suggest taking movements down to the floor or into the air?
- Could you use someone to demonstrate?
- Could you suggest at what point a change of level might occur?
- What would happen if the class was restricted to no feet on the floor, as many/few parts of the body in contact with the floor at any one time?

Dynamics
- Would the movement be clearer if executed more slowly and made bigger?
- How fast could a movement be executed?
- Could it be made faster if made smaller?
- Could pauses or holds be introduced into a sequence?
- Could certain movements be repeated to create a rhythm?
- How many repeats are effective? At what point does it become repetitive and boring?
- Could certain movements be speeded up whilst others are slowed down?
- Could you suggest a timing pattern, e.g. slow–pause–fast–very fast–stop?

Relationships
- Are the children working together or is one member of the group dominating?
- Can they trust one another sufficiently to follow someone's idea through?
- Are they nervous of physical contact?
- Could you suggest a task that would help overcome this?
- Does everyone in the group know what to do or are they simply following?
- Is all the movement in unison? Could canon, passing movements or variations be introduced?

Use of accompaniment
- Does the music help the task or is it unclear and confusing?
- Does it help the movements the pupils have selected?
- Does everyone understand when to start and when to finish?
- Is the class responding to the rhythm of the music?
- Are they adhering too strictly to the beat?
- Could they experiment with using the phrasing of the music, creating contrasting rhythms, consciously resisting the rhythm?
- How does the music affect the quality of the movement?

After the lesson

Lesson structure
- Were the tasks selected appropriate to achieve your intentions?
- Was there a balance in the kind of activities between structured teacher-led tasks and open-ended work?
- Did you revise your plan during the course of the lesson? Why? What effect did this have?
- Was there sufficient opportunity for the pupils to devise dance, individually and/or as part of a group?
- Was there sufficient opportunity to watch and talk about dance?

Responding to developments
- Was the group sufficiently enabled to explore an aspect of dance in depth?
- Were your comments appropriate? How did they affect the pupils' work?
- What ideas did the pupils initiate? How did you respond? Did you compromise or miss any creative opportunities?
- Were the pupils sufficiently enabled to create original work at their respective levels of ability?
- Was the choice of content and stimulus appropriate?

The teaching context
- Did you maximise the resource of supporting staff?
- What extraneous pressures shaped the lesson? Time? Pace? Space? Interruptions? Noise thresholds?
- Did anything unexpected arise during the lesson? How did you respond?
- What was the attitude of the pupils? How did they affect you? Did they change?

Teaching decisions
- Did you communicate instructions clearly or was there confusion?
- Did the activities contain the pupils and keep them suitably focused and on task?
- Were activities and tasks sufficiently differentiated to meet the needs of all the pupils?
- Did all the pupils demonstrate their achievements?
- How did you set up activities? By requests? Orders? Choices? Negotiation? Did you feel comfortable with this?

'Troubleshooting!' – coping with management difficulties

The following pointers have all been useful to me at times when teaching dance in a range of educational settings. Unfortunately, none are bullet-proof! Some are my own observations, some originally are those of others, notably Lowden (1989) and Sherborne (1990).

Unsuitable dance space

- Slippery floor: stress the need for care; discourage running, sliding, slithering, skidding in socks, all of which polish the floor!
- Cold floor: this will excite the children, make them fidgety and lose concentration; warm the children up with energetic activities and limit prolonged floor-based work; in severe cases, consider using mats for relationship play work and wearing plimsolls for floor-based activities.
- Cold, draughty room: this will cause children to lose concentration; again, keep them moving and allow extra layers of clothing that may be discarded.
- Airless room: if the room cannot be ventilated change the activity more frequently, allowing short 'rest' periods for relaxation and discussion; use a free-standing fan, perhaps, or consider incorporating lengths of fabric or stimuli to waft.
- Atmosphere: this may be changed by drawing curtains, switching lights on or off, using screens to define areas of the room.
- Insufficient space: adapt the classroom; work small with movement that takes up little space, such as exploring use of gesture and holding stillness in frozen images; negotiate whatever hall space is available (e.g. run a lunchtime or after school club); avoid working outside as this often proves too distracting.

Children who are unenthusiastic

- Find out what interests them, e.g. collecting current cult figures from cereal packets, pictures of footballing or pop stars in action, etc. Do images suggest ideas to be developed in movement? For example, exploit their interest in sport by considering ideas of 'winning and losing', using press photos as stimuli (i.e. developing use of gesture, and open/closed body shapes), perhaps moving in slow motion from one 'photograph' to another, involving a change of level; possibly perform to accompaniment of 'Chariots of Fire' theme (adapted from Allen and Coley, 1995a, p. 14).

● Is there a particular dance style that appeals? For example, disco dancing, break-dancing, 'Riverdance'. Use these as starting points and aim to extend their involvement in the movements and to combine steps in original ways.

● Record extracts on video of their favourite popular bands performing dance routines to accompany their singing: analyse their dance steps (volume turned down), children to select two or three to practise and perfect, then to add a new step; choreograph the routine to perform in a group.

Children who behave irresponsibly in the hall

● Avoid referring to the session as 'dance' or 'movement' unless the children are likely to be motivated if you do (dance tends to have more credibility these days!).

● Set clear boundaries on behaviour and praise appropriate behaviour.

● Play movement games to start with that will focus and challenge the children: e.g. crossing the space without using the feet, 'blind walks' (leading blindfolded partner sensitively around the space), mirror work (exactly copying a partner's actions), etc.

● Avoid any special preparations to start with: allow children to keep shoes on, and do not worry about getting changed.

● Make sure your own clothing does not inadvertently set you up for ridicule! (No shiny lycra unless you think the children will be positively impressed!)

● Consider tasks that entail observing, writing or drawing, as well as moving.

● Focus work on floor-based activities that will 'earth' the children.

● Set tasks as challenges, where pupils' strength may be put to the test in activities that demand focusing concentration; e.g. 'I bet you won't be able to undo me if I curl up like a tight parcel'.

Lack of support from staff

● Don't try to pressure or coerce colleagues: let the children be your best PR officers for dance.

● Under-state your image as a 'dancer' (avoid shiny lycra in the staff-room too!): rather, cultivate a quiet image with ordinary casual clothing, to foster the notion that 'dance is for all'.

- Recognise where colleagues *do* feel secure in dance (radio broadcast material? country dancing?). Share their interest and quietly show how you use these perhaps as starting-points, and then develop children's own ideas, perhaps adapting suggestions for follow-up work in an accompanying teachers' booklet.
- Offer to fill an assembly slot with dance in order to raise awareness and curiosity of ways of working amongst colleagues.
- Offer to run a staff workshop to enlighten colleagues; make sure activities are not too energetic, and do not involve excessive rolling around on the floor or lots of bending; respect people not wanting to work in bare feet, or complaining of bad backs; work to the strengths of supporting staff (see below)
- Collaborate with colleagues responsible for other curricular areas to devise dance work developed from topics, so that colleagues see the relevance and overlap from natural curricular links.
- Take opportunities to indicate how hard the children are working towards performing a piece of work, and how dance contributes to understanding across other areas of the curriculum: be strategic over comments about 'problem solving', 'speaking and listening' skills, developing children's cultural awareness, etc.

Children who are diffident over movement and dance

- Do not pressure children to join in at first but involve them in related observational tasks from the side of the room; for example, watching for children who are performing a particular action, maintaining a particular body shape; also perhaps providing percussion accompaniment for a dance sequence.
- Do not draw attention or make a 'special case' of the child; allow the child the opportunity to discreetly join the group when ready, without making (literally!) a song and dance of it.
- If the large space of the hall is threatening, consider screening off part of it and reducing the working space; start in a corner, rather than sitting in the middle of the room.
- Consider working from a secure 'safe place', e.g. on mats to start with, or chairs to return to.
- Perhaps develop movement work in the classroom initially before transferring it to the hall.
- Do not insist the child gets changed into dance gear.

- Ensure movement and dance themes are developed from stimuli that will capture interest (see above), developed from the familiar.
- Consider using catchy music accompaniment which will be irresistible for tapping along to; also music that is currently popular.
- Entice children into movement by capitalising on their powers of observation, e.g. 'can you *show* us the shape Susan made with her body that you said looked good – I'm not quite sure I understood you properly'.

Working with supporting staff

- Endeavour to work to colleagues' strengths and interests – are they keen to take part? Would they rather be more 'on the edge'? Would they prefer to work relatively unobtrusively, supporting a particular child?
- Explain your rationale for the lesson beforehand so that there is method to the apparent madness!
- Brief staff clearly over their function; find tactful ways to channel enthusiasm and any urge to dominate ideas.
- Make sure staff are clear how to work with children in need of physical support: support above the joint so that the child increasingly will take weight through the limb, and aim to fade out the amount of support required.
- If staff are not keen on active involvement, exploit their position on the edge: for example, involve them in assessment; ask them to observe or track particular pupils, or perhaps to operate a video camera.
- Check ahead of the lesson, to avoid embarrassment in front of the class, whether staff mind children 'doing things' to them, e.g. rolling them over, using them as a vault, etc. Are they prepared to wriggle through a human tunnel made by the children?
- Involve staff in managing stimuli (e.g. blowing up a balloon and letting it go), providing percussion accompaniment or controlling the cassette player.
- Encourage staff to work strategically amongst certain groupings, perhaps tactfully to elicit responses and suggestions from more withdrawn pupils or those with limited verbal language.
- Take time to practise with staff their ability to pose a hierarchy of questions, 'open' and 'closed', in order to maximise children's creativity and to avoid the creative process being inadvertently hi-jacked.

- Try to minimise 'traffic' through the dance space: staff may be more prepared to join in if they are confident there will be no intrusions.
- Encourage staff to dress appropriately to preserve their dignity and to enable them to respond uninhibitedly.

Children with excessive energy

- Include plenty of floor-based work to 'earth' them.
- Incorporate activities that require children to focus and channel their energy, e.g. to resist being pushed or pulled, to roll a partner over, etc.
- Include warm-up exercises that are in the form of concentration games, e.g. responding to special signals in a particular way, playing musical bumps or statues, etc.
- Work tight: minimise the dance space available, e.g. screen off part of the room, work on mats perhaps and focus on 'personal space', with small movements.
- Use movement themes that are to do with developing gesture, maintaining balances, holding stillness, etc.
- Allow them to 'let off steam' on entering the dance space; contrast with calm, still activities, so that children become aware of the ebb and flow of energy.
- Include free-flowing activities but which are reliant on contact with others, e.g. being swung from behind by a supporting adult, or swung in a blanket by peers.
- Work towards children experiencing slow, sustained movements; use accompanying music judiciously to give support and structure.

Children who avoid contact

- Children may be prepared to engage in partner or group work if it is through a medium: for example, moving with a prop between them (balloon, length of elastic, piece of material, etc); you then try removing the item so that children *imagine* it is still between them.
- Include movement experiences where they do not have to be directly 'hands on' but are nevertheless required to work alongside others, e.g. to take their place as part of the structure for the human tunnel or bridge.
- Children may be more accepting of physical contact if this is from behind initially, avoiding face to face contact: e.g. being cradled, swung, given an 'engine ride' back to back, escaping from a 'prison' when contained by their partner, etc.

- Try activities where partners are on different levels; children may be intrigued by this and make better eye contact (e.g. aeroplane rides, sliding a partner by the ankles, etc).
- Encourage role-reversal experiences: child to help adult to stand up, child to cradle adult, etc.
- Develop movement experiences where children have to learn to adjust their energy; 'pulling' (an expression of wish) may be easier to accept than 'pushing' (a more overt statement against another): e.g. sliding an adult along by wrists or ankles, rolling the adult by pulling towards, etc.
- Include free flowing activities that require the child to cling (an indication of commitment and trust), e.g. being taken for a ride astride an adult's back, an enclosed spin, a 'gibbon' carry with minimal hand support from the adult, etc.
- Ensure activities are fun and playful, so that they do not appear threatening.

Children with physical disability

- Develop questioning skills of staff to empower children to make creative decisions: use of 'closed' questions (requiring yes/no answers) as well as open questions.
- Enhance the status of a wheelchair as a means for providing interesting contrasts of levels; e.g. the power of the seated figure, as featured historically in art.
- Interpret terminology imaginatively, e.g .'travelling' to include using wheelchairs.
- Include movement experiences to foster relaxation and reduction of body tension, e.g. free-flowing experiences (possibly in a blanket) and body contact against others (being cradled, rocked, stroked, etc.).
- Include sensations of 'falling' from the side onto the back, to help reduce tension in the neck.
- Children may be offered 'hands on' experiences of being swung if they have sufficient neck control; if their tension is flaccid, however, they may still experience the free-flow by being swung in a blanket.
- Give intentionality to spontaneous movement or vocalisation and initiative so that they develop control over voluntary movement.
- Encourage children to transfer their weight onto hands and even knees (check advice from a physiotherapist first), and to develop strength in the back, neck and legs.

- Enlarge limited movement (e.g. tying lengths of ribbon to a finger).
- Enable children to experience tension against others by linking with lengths of taut elastic.
- Encourage supporting staff to make their movement an integral feature of the child's dance rather than being a 'manipulator' of limbs, e.g. curling their own body in relation to the child, to make a feature of the child's interesting body shape.
- Find ways for children to make a dance statement in relation to others, e.g. connected through stimuli (lengths of material, ribbon, whirly tubes with elastic threaded through, etc).
- Work to children's strengths: despite limited bodily movement they may nevertheless develop good knowledge and understanding about dance; they may be excellent observers of others' achievements, constructive critics, or choreographers.
- Encourage staff to 'listen' sensitively to the body reaction of pre-verbal children and those with PMLD, and to interpret and use their preferred responses in movement experiences as the basis for creating sequences in dance.

Finding music for dance

- Dance does not have to be accompanied by music. Music can elevate the work, however, and also enhance movement quality if appropriately chosen. Body percussion and use of the voice to accompany dance can be very effective.
- If using pre-recorded music, beware of the tempo of the particular recording; sometimes the same piece can be a particularly fast rendition!
- Be ready to adapt, to fit (literally!) the pace of the children; for example, 'Swing' is slower than original 'Boogie Woogie', and may be better suited to beginners at Lindy Hop (Jazz).
- Music should be selected to match the movement/dance needs in question, *not* the other way round (i.e. not starting with the music, and then thinking of some dance to go with it).
- There are a growing number of teachers' packs for music to support National Curriculum teaching which include tapes with extracts of music for listening. Many of these are ideal for dance accompaniment, as very often they have been selected to exemplify a clear structure, to evoke a particular quality or to suggest an idea with contrasting features.

- Certain types of music have a rambling structure and will be suitable to accompany children's dance, where keeping within a clear pulse (beat) is not essential. For example, Ragtime will lend itself to dance where use of gesture is a particular movement theme (the 'silent movie effect').
- Strongly atmospheric music (e.g. the synthesised electronic work of Philip Glass or Brian Eno) may lend itself to enhancing quality of movement, without imposing a specific beat, but where clear phrasing may be a feature.
- Soothing atmospheric music may have an important relaxing effect on children; for example, at the end of a session or to accompany movement work with children with PMLD (e.g. 'Antarctica', by Vaughan Williams).
- Look for extracts that have a clear structure with strongly contrasting sections. For example, Saint-Saëns' 'Carnival of the Animals' features several evocative pieces, all with clear patterns, such as 'Hens and Cocks' (sustained sinewy sounds of fowl pecking and scratching about, followed by rapid scurrying).
- Let children compose their own original music to accompany dance. For example, 'Rainforest' music (wooden/ethnic percussion) to communicate vegetation growing and living in harmony, followed by a section to convey felling of trees (solo drum roll and cymbal crash), followed by a final section (regeneration? or silence?) – (see Wills and Peter, 1996).
- Use contrasting percussion to accompany simple changes of action, to enhance the meaning of the statement; e.g. tambourine – chime bar – guiro, to accompany three different ways of bouncing.
- Live accompaniment may be adapted to fit with the dance, unlike pre-recorded music.
- Be aware of when to introduce music accompaniment as it will always impose in some way: children may have devised a piece and be forced to adapt it to fit the music (which can be important learning in itself). Alternatively, children may be made aware of the music from the outset; however, this should be put to one side while they are concentrating on developing the movement content, and reintroduced when children are working towards their composition.
- Using music with a strong pulse or current popular music may motivate children to engage in dance who might otherwise be indifferent or disinterested. For example, music by 'Art of Noise', or 'The Penguin Café Orchestra'; catchy numbers such as 'Popcorn', etc.
- Playing certain music in the background may help elevate the status of basic movement work with older pupils (e.g. opera, or South American pan pipes)

Lesson Plans

Pre/Lower Key Stage 1

Example 1: 'Lycra'

Topic:	'myself' – body awareness
Movement themes:	action – stretching; body shape
Stimulus:	large piece of stretchy lycra fabric; 'body bag' made from piece of lycra stitched into a sack form
Accompaniment	'Hens and Cocks' (Saint-Saëns' 'Carnival of the Animals')

Establishing theme:
- Group sitting in circle, adults/carers supporting children from behind, as necessary
- Introduce lycra, everyone to hold on to it; use voice to show how we can make it s-t-r-e-t-c-h (everyone pull)

Warm up:
- Sing song to accompany everyone holding on to lycra, and swaying side-to-side
- Stretching up-and-down
- Stretching forwards-and-backwards (everyone lean back, still holding on)
- Possibly try the same exercises, but *without* the lycra.
modification: minimal adult support in order to achieve
extension: controlled stretching, until fully extended

Development and exploration:

- Children in turn to crawl (or be placed) under the lycra, while everyone holds lycra down over them to make an unusual form. Can we work out where (Susan's) knee is? Toe? Elbow?
- Children under lycra to push into the lycra using voluntary movement, to make a new shape
- Slide children along on lycra
- Give children a swing in the lycra (a stretchy hammock!)

modification: adult support in order to achieve

extension: introduce contrasts in speed, level, tension, pathway, direction, etc

Selecting and creating:

- Children dotted around the room, making a low level shape (lying, sitting), supporting staff to enlarge their shape
- Individuals in turn perform an AB dance (two distinctly contrasting sections): sequence two or three stretchy shapes with the lycra, then be slid as fast as possible amongst the others on the lycra
- Observers to recall shapes made by individual dancers

modification: adult and child make shapes 'as one'

extension: child invents and holds unusual body shape

Pre/Lower Key Stage 1

Example 2: 'Worms Wiggle'

Topic:	animals
Movement themes:	action – wiggling; body – whole body awareness; managing weight on the floor
Stimulus:	whirly tube; story book 'Worms Wiggle' (Pelham and Foreman, 1988)
Accompaniment	guiro (scraper), drum and beater

Establishing theme:

- Read story 'Worms Wiggle' (pop up book of animals performing characteristic actions)
- Look at worm wiggling: show children wiggling action, using whirly tube

Warm up:

- Everyone sitting in circle, children supported from behind as necessary by adults/carers; sing song 'Wiggly Woo', wriggling every time they hear the words 'Wiggly Woo' or 'wriggle'
- Wiggle fingers, then toes; contast with stiff, straight fingers and toes
- Wiggle trunk; contrast with stillness
- Curl up, and open up into a long wiggly shape along ground
- Those that can, stand up: wiggle legs and arms; make wiggle shape by twisting to look behind, keeping feet still

modification: minimal adult support in order to achieve

extension: performing tasks with flexibility of the trunk

Development and exploration:

- Everyone to have a whirly; take it for a wiggle: on the spot, around the room, up high, down low
- Children to go for a wiggle on their tummies and/or backs
- In twos (some children to partner one another, others to be partnered by an adult): take partner for a slide, 'feeding in' a wiggle, and following a wiggly pathway
- Two staff to help children in turn to do giant wiggle: support child on either side by forearm and under arm
- Staff/carers make human tunnel ('burrow'!), 'worms' to wiggle through

modification: children to be partnered by staff; slid on a blanket

extension: responsible children to partner one another independently; controlled flexibility of the trunk

Selecting and creating:

- Solo 'Wiggly Woo' dance: teacher-led improvised dance, between moments of silence
- Start curled up shape (silence), open into long shape, wiggle along floor on tummies or backs (to guiro), bird coming: curl up small back into burrow ! (drum beat, silence)
- Perform in two halves, observers to watch for impressive wiggly bodies of 'worms', and those 'worms' curled up tightly

modification: adult and child make shapes 'as one' ; child to be slid on blanket

extension: perform with flexibility of trunk, contrasts in body shape and speed

Pre/Lower Key Stage 1

Example 3: 'Balloons'

Topic: 'things that fly'
Movement themes: action – bouncing, rolling; body – round and long
                      shapes
Stimulus: balloon
Accompaniment   swannee whistle, chime bars, maraca

Establishing theme:
- Watch balloon: what does it do? (blow it up – get bigger, let it go – shrink)
- Watch action of balloon: throw it down onto ground so that it bounces, then rolls and comes to a standstill; use this as basic structure for dance

Warm up:
- Curl up and open up hands, as balloon inflates; shake out, as balloon shrinks (accompany with swannee whistle 'growing' sounds)
- Curl up body (tuck in knees), open out into big, wide round shape; shake out as balloon shrinks
- Squatting, up close with everyone bunched together, inflate balloon: everyone to open up slowly and move back holding hands, to make a giant group balloon

modification: minimal adult support in order to achieve; adult and child make 'balloon shape' together

extension: decide on shape of balloon (round or long and thin) – hold shape

Exploration and development:
- On hands and feet, take weight on hands and tuck up feet in little bunny jumps: travel round the room
- Move onto little legs (squatting): find a range of ways of bouncing round the room (explosive jumps, etc.)
- Practise bouncing on adult's back (sit astride or lying across), several adult's together if pupil is large
- Use grown up (or older peer on hands and knees): practise bouncing with little steps, learning onto adult's back for support
- Use grown up or older peer to practise bouncy jumps: carer to extend forearms, face up, child to use for support, leaning on the carer's arms

- In threes, two adults support child by forearm and under arm, to help child to bounce
- Rolling in twos: roll each other from lying on their side, on to their back again (watch for signs of relaxation)
- Rolling in twos: hold hands above head and perform a double roll on the floor, in a long thin balloon shape
- Individually, roll in different ways round the room (round, curled up, stretched out, open-and-closed body shapes, etc.)

modification: child partnered by adult; achieving bouncing and rolling with support

extension: responsible pupils to partner one another independently

Selecting and creating

- Improvised, teacher-led ABC structure (perform in two halves, so they have a chance to observe their partner)
- Small starting position: slowly inflate into a shape (round? long and thin?); travel round room, maintaining 'balloon' shape in bouncing action, change into a rolling balloon action, balloon comes to a stop
- Observers to recall the shape of their partner's 'balloon', using appropriate vocabulary/signs; also to watch for light, springy bounces like a balloon

modification: adult to support child in role, in the context of the dance 'inflate' and play with 'balloon' (roll over, spin, etc.)

extension: poise and elevation in bouncing, emphasis on 'light' quality, maintaining body shape; controlled, fluent rolling

Upper Key Stage 1

Example 1: 'Backs'

Topic: 'myself'
Movement themes: body – awareness of backs (trunk); developing partner work
Stimulus:
Accompaniment   tambourine, wood block, cabasa

Establishing theme:

- Everyone sitting in circle: feel your back (spine, knobbly bits, wobbly bits, squidgy bits!)
- Feel the back of the person next to you

- Sit back to back and let your backs say hallo (warm!)

Warm up:
- Hug knees (curl back, put chin on knees): open up slowly into a big, wide stretch
- Quickly curl up again, repeat
- Quickly curl up, gently tip off balance using toes to push, without losing balance
- Maintain curled up shape: tip side to side, forwards and backwards, round and round
- Maintain curled up shape: roll back onto floor and sit up again
- Curl up sideways on floor: open out into long stretch
- Curl up on knees; adult to lift and carry to different part of the circle
- Curled up on knees: uncurl back, to stretch upwards as tall as possible
- Give a good shake, feel back wiggling

modification: child to achieve flexibility of spine with adult support
extension: controlled extension and flexion of the spine to stretch and bend

Development and exploration:
- Move along floor on backs in different ways; using hands, then not using hands but feet only (pick interesting examples, for children to learn by copying one another's ideas)
- In twos: roll partner gently onto their backs, from lying sideways
- In twos: slide partner along floor on their back – feed in wiggle (wiggly backs)
- In twos: one to make a strong back (on hands and knees), other to use partner as vault: place hands on partner's back, and practise jumping
- In twos: sit back to back, move partner along floor using back ('engine' ride – see figure 3.21)
- In twos: slow motion see-saw, gently lowering partner so that the back is in full contact with the floor

modification: child to be partnered by adult
extension: responsible pupils to partner one another independently

Selecting and creating:
- Solo dance: ABC structure (perform in two halves, the other half watching their partners: what actions do they do?)
- Children to link three movements, three different ways of moving on their backs, as smoothly as possible
- Clear starting and finishing position, curled back or straight back?

- Observers to recall and describe their partner's chosen actions

modification: a partner dance, child working with adult; possibly a 'copy cat' dance, taking turns to lead

extension: emphasis on smooth transitions, clear changes in time with the accompaniment

Upper Key Stage 1

Example 2: 'Tigers'

Topic:	zoos, animals
Movement themes:	actions – stalking; body shape – big/little contrasts; transferring weight
Stimulus:	reproduction of paintings of tiger(s) (e.g. by Rousseau)
Accompaniment	'March of the Lions' (Saint Saëns' 'Carnival of the Animals'); tambourine

Establishing theme:
- Listen to extract of music: does any part of the music remind them of an animal? why? (roaring sound!)
- Show picture by Rousseau (or other artist) of tiger
- What do they know about what tigers do? how do they move?
- Elicit action words from children, translate into movement terms; e.g 'roaring' to be big mouth, big shape

Warm up:
- Everyone sitting in circle, legs out in front of them: show paws (fists, with palms facing downwards)
- Slowly stretch out 'claws' one at a time, stretch them up high, and around
- Quickly curl up 'paws', repeat
- Curl up toes, stretch out
- Take weight onto hands behind on floor, lift feet to trace shapes in the air with other 'paws'
- Curl up, lying on side, slowly open out into a stretch (to accompaniment of tambourine shaking)
- Curl up on hands and knees, slowly open out into a stretch (extend limbs one at a time)
- Curl up on hands and knees, open out into a standing up stretch, reaching paws as high as possible

modification: minimal adult support in order to achieve

extension: controlled extension and flexion, with maximum flexibility

Development and exploration:
- Travel round room slowly on hands and knees, experiment with forwards, backwards, round and round
- Emphasise lifting paws high and placing them down silently – idea of 'stalking' (low level)
- Move to standing: go for a walk with high knees and low knees; where can your knees take you?
- Emphasise paw shapes with hands held at shoulder height, and lifting knees high and placing feet silently – idea of 'stalking' (high level)

modification: travelling forwards on different levels as quietly as possible

extension: controlled lifting and placing of feet in different directions, achieving elevation and poise, with appropriate stalking 'tiger' quality

Selecting and creating
- Teacher-led class dance: ABABAB repeated pattern to match stalking/roaring sections in musical accompaniment
- Starting position (sleeping tiger): wake up, stretching limbs to end up on hands and knees to introductory section of the music
- Stalking on low level (hands and knees): turn to someone and make a large roaring shape; stalking on high level (standing): turn to someone and make a large roaring shape; hold large roar with everyone together in centre of the room.
- Perform dance in two halves: observers to watch for those who remind them of tigers; why?

modification: changing actions to match changes in the accompanying music; use of picture cues – tiger stalking, tiger roaring

extension: emphasis on expressing 'tiger' quality – darting, intent eyes, intimidating movements – bound but light

Upper Key Stage 1

Example 3: 'Drunken Sailor'

Topic: water/transport
Movement themes: actions – walking in rhythm, hopping, gesture; relationships – working in pairs

Stimulus: pictures of sailors peforming hornpipe; tape
Accompaniment   'What shall we do with the drunken sailor', pre-
                          recorded on tape; tambour

Establishing theme:
- Listen to recording on tape: do they recognise it? Explain origin of sea shanties (i.e. working songs, to help sailors do their work; what jobs did they do?); show pictures of sailors in action
- Listen again, clapping along, clapping hands above head when they hear 'hooray and *hup* she rises'

Warm up:
- Sitting in circle, feel and rub feet: literally warm them up!
- Make sounds on the floor with feet: loud, quiet; different parts of the foot
- Stand up: keep feet flat on floor, sag knees, swinging arms
- Standing tall, peel foot off the floor (transferring weight onto one foot at a time), replacing foot quietly with toes pointing down
- Contrast by stamping feet from side to side (left-right) to steady 1-2 beat on tambour

modification: adult support in order to achieve
extension: controlled stretching; exaggerated rhythmic transferring of weight

Development and exploration
- Stand still: teach legs to walk
- Walk toes – middle bit – heels, bringing up knees
- Try heels – middle bit – toes
- Go for a stamp around the room: experiment with different directions, stamping forwards, backwards and round and round
- Try stamping around the room, and put in a hop if possible; try with accompaniment, hopping to 'hooray and *hup* she rises'
- In twos: face each other, one extending forearms to support the other: practise hopping, using partner for support
- Think of actions related to jobs on board ship; stand on spot and practise: climbing rigging, leaning on rail, steering ship, sweeping the deck, etc.

modification: concentrate on stamping action with adult support; wheel-chair users to concentrate on arm gestures with adult support
extension: responsible pupils to partner one another independently; co-ordinating arm actions with stamping, and including a hop consistently in the appropriate place

Selecting and creating

- Organise class into two lines, with pairs facing each other and room between them
- Teacher-led verse-chorus dance:
  - For introductory verse (What shall we do with the drunken sailor?): stamp with the music, hands on raised elbows as if leaning on ship's rail
  - Chorus ('Hooray and hup she rises'): pairs to stamp towards one another for eight counts, hands behind in small of back; meet in middle and back for eight to complete the chorus (put in a hop on *'hup'*); step-step-step-hop
  - For each verse, copy cat in turns: one to mime a 'sailor' action, and partner to copy (or teacher calls out an action)
- Dancers to recall and describe what they did

modification: child to partner adult; wheelchair users may take their place in the line, with their 'carer' performing the steps

extension: emphasis on clarity and variety of actions, and matching actions with the tempo of the accompanying music

Lower Key Stage 2

Example 1: 'Robots'

Topic:	space
Movement themes:	actions – turning, holding stillness; dynamics – bound, direct movement; relationships – working in pairs
Stimulus:	space helmet or pictures of robot or wind-up mechanical robot toy
Accompaniment	'We are the robots' (by Kraftwerk), pre-recorded on tape; vibraslap

Establishing theme:

- Listen to music, discuss 'robotics' street dance (possibly watch on video).
- Watch mechanical toy in action, elicit appropriate action word vocabulary

Warm up:

Sitting in circle:

- Knees: tuck in, stretch out slowly

- Elbows: touch knees, floor, person next to you
- Head: drop and lift from side to side; contrast with floppy head, circle and lift
- Shoulders: lift and drop, circle, quick shrugging, alternate shrugging
- Back: sit straight with a long back; drop the head, sit up slowly, arching back

Standing:
- Wave, 'shake off' feet, one at a time (transferring weight)
- Slowly lift knee, keeping foot at right angle, turn knee out, slowly lower (repeat for other knee)
- Raise elbows so that parallel with shoulder, forearms dangling – rotate and extend forearms

modification: minimal adult support in order to achieve
extension: emphasis especially on controlled, sustained action

Development and exploration
- Travel round the room with stiff legs; teach legs to walk by bending knees
- Go for a 'silly walk', wherever your knee takes you (flowing, smooth action on different levels)
- Contrast with 'silly walk' but with 'pause button' repeatedly put on, so that it becomes jerky. How high can you raise knees? What are your arms doing? Which directions can you go in?
- In twos: support partner whilst they practise raising and turning out knees slowly and jerkily

modification: following a partner (adult?), imitating actions
extension: emphasis on controlled elevation of knees, maintaining balance with poise, and combining with arm actions

Selecting and creating
- Find three jerky robot-like actions; practise, then show them to partner
- In twos: choose one of each other's actions, then agree on a third; practise the actions together, several times over, so that the sequence becomes fluent
- Devise a partner dance, possibly including a chair (change of level); how are the robots moving in relation to one another?
- Repeat sequence three times over, then hold finishing position ('batteries run out!') until everyone has stopped
- Half the class to perform at a time: target certain children to watch particular pairs, and recall and describe what they did; what was particularly effective ('how did the dancers convince you they were robots?')

modification: 'copy cat' dance, partnering adult or peer, taking turns to lead

extension: include additional challenges to stretch certain pupils: dance must include (e.g.) robots moving away from one another at some point; also, one moving and the other moving on the spot.

Lower Key Stage 2

Example 2: 'Theseus and the Minotaur' (adapted from Allen and Coley, 1995a)

Topic:	the Greeks
Movement themes:	actions – performing simple traditional dance step; relationships – developing strength and stability (controlling energy 'against' partner); dynamics – tempo (fast/slow)
Stimulus:	story of Theseus and the Minotaur; pictures of Greek vases, showing figures; Greek artifacts with 'key' design
Accompaniment	'Zorba's Dance', pre-recorded on tape; tambour and beater

Establishing theme:
- Read story of Theseus and the Minotaur: what are reactions? Show influence of 'labyrinth' on Greek 'key' design; show pictures of Greek heroes and incidents from stories depicted on vases
- Introduce ideas for dance: labyrinth idea (spiral shapes), being strong and brave, weird monster shapes and expressions

Warm up:
- Walk round the room without bumping into anyone. How fast? How slowly? In a frightened way? In a brave way?
- Walk round the room tracing a spiral shape
- Join up with a partner and play 'follow my leader'; change levels (high, down low), tracing spiral shapes
- Join up with another pair to play 'follow my leader' in fours

modification: child to partner adult or responsible peer

extension: emphasis on quality of movement to convey moods and feelings; contrasts in levels, maintaining posture

Development and exploration
- Teach 'grapevine' step as whole class (see chapter 6)
- Develop 'grapevine' step so that the whole class traces a spiral shape, following teacher's lead
- Break into smaller groupings (half the class at a time?): practise spirals, maintaining 'grapevine' step, changing over leader; practise with the music, getting faster
- In twos, find a strong, stable position on the floor (rocks, tent-pegged, etc), test how well stuck partner is
- Try finding strong stable positions kneeling and standing (more precarious: foster a sense of responsibility, not to push partner totally off balance), test partner again
- Show one another strong stable positions with the same movement quality, but now *without* physical contact

modification: child to partner adult or responsible peer

extension: child to partner more vulnerable peer (to challenge their sensitivity in adjusting energy)

Selecting and creating
Relate the story of Theseus and the Minotaur in dance:
- Trace the 'labyrinth' in groups, performing the grapevine step, quickening with the music
- At the point where the music becomes unmanageably fast, break quickly to find partner: sequence 'brave' positions facing each other (A = Theseus, B = Minotaur), holding stillness (going against the music), changing position (to a different level) when they hear the tambour (teacher to play intermittent single beat, over the rapid tempo of the music)
- Half the class to perform at a time (possibly target certain children to watch particular pairs); observers to watch for convincing brave 'Theseus' positions and frightening 'Minotaur' shapes (why were they effective?); also how precisely groups conveyed the labyrinth in unison

modification: child to partner adult or responsible peer in imitative 'copy cat' dance, taking turns to lead

extension: devise a dance in a group (threes or fours, to create group Minotaur shapes (weird, fantastical) and a group Theseus

Lower Key Stage 2

Example 3: 'Mondrian'

Topic:	'colour and light'
Movement themes:	actions – combining and performing movements with control; using actions along pathways
Stimulus:	selection of reproductions by the artist Mondrian, featuring arrangements of oblongs in primary colours (red, blue, yellow), white, black and grey
Accompaniment	'Boogie Woogie' extracts (e.g. by Louis Jordan); alternatively 'Peter Gunn' (by the Art of Noise)

Establishing theme:
• Look at reproductions by Mondrian: invite comments, regarding arrangement of shapes, use of colour
• Decide on a code, matching a colour to a different type of action:

blue	–	travelling ('going')
red	–	jumping
yellow	–	turning
white	–	holding stillness (balancing)
grey	–	gesture
black	–	stopping

• Explain that we are going to dance the colours

Warm up:
• On the signal of a tambour beat, run into a space and make a shape: (e.g.) with a particular body part nearest the ceiling, in contact with the ground, in contact with another person, in contact with a stipulated number of people, etc.
• Perform a range of actions, matching movement to eight sets of eight counts: e.g. bouncing knees, moving on knees, travelling using knees, stretching with knees out straight (repeat)
• Choose a partner: keep the person in mind and aim to get as near to them as possible (or as far away as possible), whilst having to change direction on the 8th beat of a drum (e.g. '1, 2, 3, 4, 5, 6, 7 – Turn!')
modification: working alongside a partner throughout (supporting adult or friend)
extension: emphasis on originality in shape, and matching actions with tempo, maintaining control over body shape, and including arm actions

Development and exploration:

• Choose an action (trawl ideas from the children): perform in contrasting ways: (e.g.) slowly then quickly, holding tension (e.g. stretching) then shaking out, moving from high to low and vice versa (e.g. stretching along the ground, then stretching up high); different directions; performing precise actions contrasting with sinewy ones (e.g. swaying both arms from side to side, then punching the air with each arm in turn from high to low) etc.

• Ensure an example of jumping, turning, travelling

• In twos: one child to make a secure, stable, shape; partner to test if it's 'stuck tight' by pushing or pulling

• Experiment with secure, stable shapes on different levels (standing, kneeling, sitting, lying down)

modification: child to partner supporting adult or responsible peer

extension: challenge pupils to categorise action words (e.g. 'slithering', 'twirling', 'bounding', etc.) and select from these to practise actions (this could be at random: picking cards from piles of 'jumping' words, 'turning' words, 'going' words, 'gesture' words, 'stopping' words, etc.)

Selecting and creating:

• Partner dance: use a Mondrian reproduction as a script for a dance; isolate a pathway through the painting, and use the coloured oblongs to suggest which type of action is required (size of oblong to influence the length of time the action is performed, or the size of the action?)

• Agree a way of jumping, turning, going, stopping and a gesture etc. to match to the colours involved

• Decide how they will 'travel' through the painting: one after the other? from opposite directions? in unison? away from one another?

• Emphasise poise, control and elevation in their actions

• Perform several pairs at a time (not too many, otherwise clarity may be lost)

• Observers to watch a particular pair: recall what they did and what was particularly effective/interesting in their dance; if part of the dance was to be changed which bit could be improved and how?

modification: have separate coloured cards available, that may be placed on the floor (literally) to support pupils in planning their pathway; partnering an adult or responsible peer and dancing in unison, or following a lead

extension: turn a corner in the painting, then return by the same route; make actions more complex, co-ordinating changes in combined arm and leg actions

Upper Key Stage 2/3

Example 1: 'Riverdance'

Topic:	Ireland
Movement themes:	actions – performing complex, combined actions (transferring weight); body – posture; traditional dances of the British Isles
Stimulus:	video of 'Riverdance'; coloured toy building bricks
Accompaniment	slow Irish jig (from soundtrack?), pre-recorded on tape; tambour and beater

Establishing theme:
- Watch video of 'Riverdance': discuss technique; what are the features? (everyone in unison, keeping in time, straight body, small foot movements)
- Listen to tape of Irish jig: how many times does the tune repeat? (use coloured bricks to notate the pattern)

Warm up:
- Stand on the spot, rotate the feet in turn (transfer weight)
- Peel each foot off the floor, lifting knees and pointing toes to replace (repeat to slow steady beat)
- Push toes flat on the floor, raising heel, to count of four, swap to other foot for four beats (repeat)
- Feet flat on floor, sag knees, keeping bottom tucked in, to count of eight, stretching up tall on eighth beat
- Slowly drop down, curling over back to eight counts
- Perform eight 'bobs', keeping toes on floor, lifting heels lightly
- Perform eight small springy jumps, keeping with the beat; perform 'round the clock' (quarter turns)

modification: concentrating on actions, stopping when the accompaniment ceases
extension: emphasis on slickness in transitions, nimble quality

Development and exploration
- Teach step – step – step – hop, alternating feet for each step, repeating over and over again
- Go for a walk, exaggerating a wild shape every time they hop; experiment with levels, directions
- Return to line, facing teacher: teach step – step – step – hop, this time

performing 'round the clock' so that dancers do a quarter turn to start each phrase facing a new direction
- Practise with a partner so that steps match, this time keeping body very straight

modification: concentrate on step pattern, partnering adult or friend
extension: partnering a peer who is not from usual friendship group; emphasis on clarity, precision and posture

Selecting and creating
- Whole class dance, in a long line: devise a sequence dancing steps on the spot (repeat), moving forwards for four, moving backwards for four, then 'round the clock' to complete the phrase
- In groups choreograph a new routine to fit the phrase
- This may be extended with a more complex step pattern, performed double-time (work through the same lesson structure, but with the more complex steps): step-hop step-hop step-step step-hop
- Perform in two halves: observers to comment on those dancers successfully synchronising their moves; what was particularly effective? why? (contrasts in pathways, directions, patterns, etc)

modification: work in small groups (with adult or responsible peer strategically placed), use the simple step pattern, but add arm actions
extension: devise a group dance (in threes or fours) using the complex step, with some challenges: (e.g. starting small and getting larger, where dancers change places, where there's a change in the group shape (triangle? circle? line?) including arm actions

Upper Key Stage 2/3

Example 2: The Rainforest (adapted from Allen and Coley, 1995a)

Topic:	the Environment
Movement themes:	relationships – developing group balances and shapes to convey ideas of 'harmony';
Stimulus:	protest posters to 'Save the Rainforest' (commercial or made by the children)
Accompaniment	pupils' own music, conveying a narrative: everything living in harmony, motifs to represent certain creatures, destruction of vegetation, possible regeneration – live or pre-recorded on tape

Establishing theme:
- Look at posters of the Rainforest. Discuss the implications of its destruction.
- Agree a narrative to explain what is happening; 'score' a dance script, using symbols, pictures or words

Warm up:
- On the signal of a tambour beat, run into a space and make a shape: (e.g.) with a particular body part nearest the ceiling, in contact with the ground, in contact with another person, in contact with a stipulated number of people, etc.
- Slow, sustained stretching and curling up, matching movement to eight sets of eight counts, alternating fluently, varying the direction, level and which part of the body is leading
- Contrast with fast, jerky 'shaking out' of arms and feet from high to low, front to back, to eight counts, changing swiftly from right to left
  modification: stretching and curling up in stages, 'freezing' mid-way; 'shaking out' one side first, then the other
  extension: counting to eight inside head, pacing extension and flexion of the body; transferring weight deftly to 'shake out' alternating right and left sides

Development and exploration:
- In twos: sit facing one another, gripping by the wrists: perform a see-saw in slow motion, relaxing back the head and lowering partner in turn
- Develop see-saw principle from knees and standing; try also with one hand, making a shape with the other
- Counter-balance in standing position: sit down together, stand up again, hold balance half way; develop into a spin
- In twos stand up and sit down back to back
- In fours: make a group shape; keep feet still, but build in a sense of movement; practise starting small and growing into the shape, then swaying
- In twos: one to lie down on side, partners in turn roll one another over, partner encouraging to relax and 'let go' of own weight
- In twos: experiment with different ways of rolling each other over (round shape, long thin shape)
- In twos: experiment with different ways of rolling over in unison (joined at the feet, holding hands, one next to the other, etc.)
- In twos: one pushes the other gently so that partner practises falling

and rolling from different levels, from sitting, then kneeling, then standing

modification: partnering an adult or responsible peer

extension: partnering a more vulnerable peer; working with peers other than usual friends

Selecting and creating:

- In fours or more: create a group dance to convey the fate of the Rainforest: small seeds growing into vegetation with fantastical shapes, vegetation being felled, possible rejuvenation
- Emphasise conviction, importance of expression, commitment
- Encourage contrasts in levels and body tension
- Observers to interpret a group's dance: what was happening? how could they tell?

modification: partner dance; alternatively adult or responsible child placed strategically in group to support particular child

extension: include solo parts to convey a particular creature that moves amongst the vegetation; lumberjack felling vegetation; create an alternative ending

Upper Key Stage 2/3

Example 3: 'The Card Players' (adapted from Allen and Coley, 1995b)

Topic:	sport, pastimes
Movement themes:	actions – gesture; creating characters
Stimulus:	reproduction of Cezanne's painting 'The Card Players'; pack of cards
Accompaniment	extract from 'The Pecherine Rag' (Scott Joplin)

Establishing theme:

- Look at reproduction: discuss the images (what are they are doing? who are they? what can we tell about the two men? etc.)
- Extract movement ideas contained in the painting: gestures, shuffling, fanning of cards, ideas of randomness or canon (cards being dealt one after the other).

Warm up:

- Everyone to sit on chairs around the edge of the room: on a signal (e.g. duck call), walk into the middle of the room and greet one another in a particular way (teacher to call out e.g. 'tired', 'angry', 'irritable', etc.); retreat to the edge of the room again on contrasting signal (e.g. triangle sounding), still in character
- Move around the room as fast as possible, changing direction on cue from teacher (e.g. tambour beats) and darting amongst other people without bumping
- On the signal of a tambour beat, run into a space and make a shape: (e.g.) with a particular body part nearest the ceiling, in contact with the ground, in contact with another person, in contact with a stipulated number of people, etc.

modification: target particular children to move according to familiar emotions, 'sad', 'happy', 'cross', etc.

extension: target particular children to move according to more complex emotions, 'proud', 'haughty', etc.

Development and exploration:

- Sit on chairs at edge of room: turn chair to face a partner: look at picture of 'The Card Players' and take up pose of one of the characters
- Take up a new pose ('what does the character do next?'); freeze as if in a new picture
- Stand up and walk in character in to a third pose; freeze as if in a new picture, then return to chair, still in character
- In twos, practise the three gestures in sequence, repeating until fluent
- From chairs, agree a way of moving into groups of six (in canon?)
- In sixes, devise a way of representing shuffling cards (e.g. standing in a line, one behind the other, take it in turns to move to the front)
- In sixes, make fan shapes

modification: child to mirror partner's gestures; child to be anchor point within the group – holding stillness, whilst others move around

extension: emphasis on facial expression to convey feelings of character, contrasted with blankness of playing card; contrast between holding stillness and purposeful action in character

Selecting and creating

- Whole class dance (performed in two halves): pairs of card players sitting on chairs around edge of room, performing their sequence of poses four times over (hold stillness in character, if they finish ahead of others); on agreed cue (point in the music?) move in 'blank' characterless way into group lines; perform alternating shuffling then fan shapes; invent an ending (e.g. cards being flung? slammed down?)

● Emphasise contrasts between characters of card players and 'characterless' playing cards; encourage children to repeat their sequences as accurately as possible, to develop their movement memory (Allen and Coley, 1995b)

● Observers to comment on characterisation: who was particularly convincing and why? Describe the shapes made to convey 'shuffling' and 'fanning'; what happened at the end of the dance? how could they tell?

modification: child to mirror actions of partner and group members as accurately as possible; repeat same 'shuffling' and 'fan' shapes

extension: devise new characters playing cards; e.g. extend into four characters playing bridge; perform different alternating 'shuffling' and 'fan' shapes, with fluency in transitions, flexibility in movements and clarity of characterisation

Bibliography

Allen, A and Coley, J (1995a) *Dance for All 2*. London: David Fulton.

Allen, A and Coley, J (1995b) *Dance for All 3*. London: David Fulton.

Allen, A and Coley, J (1996) *Dance for All 1*. London: David Fulton.

Anderson, E (1987) 'Movement Education for Children with Severe Learning Difficulties', *British Journal of Physical Education*, vol 18, no 5, 199–200.

Arts Council of Great Britain (1993) *Dance in Schools*. London: Arts Council.

Athey, C (1990) *Extending Thought in Young Children*. London: Paul Chapman.

Barthorpe, T (1992) *Differentiation – Eight Ideas for the Classroom*. Scunthorpe: Desktop Publications.

Baxter, C (1991) *Moving into Dance*. Norwich: Norfolk Educational Press.

Best, D (1985) *Feeling and Reason in the Arts*. London: Allen and Unwin.

Brinson, P 1991) *Dance as Education*. London: Falmer.

Bruner, J (1986) *Actual Minds: Possible Worlds*. Cambridge, Mass.: Harvard University Press.

Collis, M and Lacey, P (1996) *Interactive Approaches to Teaching*. London: David Fulton.

Cratty, B (1975) *Remedial Motor Activity for Children*. Philadelphia: Lea and Febiger.

Cullingford Agnew, S and Griffiths, B (1990) 'What's in it for our Kids? Sherborne Movement – an Approach for all Pupils', *Drama and Dance*, Winter, 1990, 24–25.

DES (1992) *Physical Education in the National Curriculum*. London: HMSO.

DFE (1995) *Physical Education in the National Curriculum*. London: HMSO.

Gerry, S and Dibbo, J (1995) 'Caring and Sharing: physical education, therapy and Sherborne Developmental Movement', *CORE*, vol 19, no 2.

Gough, M (1993) *In Touch with Dance*. Lancaster: Whitehorn Books.

Groves, L (1979) *Physical Education for Special Needs*. Cambridge: Cambridge University Press.

Gulbenkian Foundation (1982) *The Arts in Schools*. London: Calouste Gulbenkian Foundation.

Harrison, K (1986) *Look! Look! What I Can Do!* London: BBC.

Harrison, K (1993) *Let's Dance*. London: Hodder and Stoughton.

Hill, C (1991) *Down to Earth – literally!* London: London Drama.

Hobson, R P (1993) *Autism and the Development of Mind.* London: Erlbaum.

Holimann, M and Weikart, D (1995) *Educating Young Children.* Michigan: High Scope Press.

Jordan, R and Powell, S (1995) *Understanding and Teaching Children with Autism.* Chichester: Wiley.

Kephart, N (1971) *The Slow Learner in the Classroom.* Columbus, Ohio: Charles E Merrill

Laban, R (1948, reprinted 1975) *Modern Educational Dance.* Plymouth: Macdonald and Evans.

Levete, G (1982) *No Handicap to Dance.* London: Souvenir Press.

Lewis, A (1991) *Primary Special Needs and the National Curriculum.* London: Routledge.

Lowden, M (1989) *Dancing to Learn.* Lewes: Falmer.

Meier, W (1979) 'Meeting Special Needs through Movement and Dance Drama', *Therapeutic Education,* vol 7, no 1, 27–33.

Mitchell, S (1994) 'Some Implications of the High/Scope Curriculum and the Education of Children with Learning Difficulties' in Coupe O'Kane, J and Smith, B (eds.) *Taking Control.* London: David Fulton.

Nind, M and Hewitt, D (1994) *Access to Communication.* London: David Fulton.

North, M (1972 & 1990) *Personality Assessment through Movement.* Plymouth: Northcote House.

North, M (1973 & 1990) *Movement and Dance Education.* Plymouth: Northcote House.

OFSTED (1994) *Handbook for the Inspection of Schools.* London: OFSTED

Payne, H (1990) 'The Integration of Psycho-Emotional Growth', *British Journal of Physical Education,* vol 21, no 4, 407.

Payne, H (1992) *Dance Movement Therapy: Theory and Practice.* London: Routledge.

Pelham, D and Foreman, M (1988) *Worms Wiggle.* London: Carnival.

Peter, M J (1994) *Drama for All.* London: David Fulton.

Peter, M J (1995) *Making Drama Special.* London: David Fulton.

Peter, M J (1996a) *Art For All 1: The Framework.* London: David Fulton.

Peter, M J (1996b) *Art For All 2: The Practice.* London: David Fulton.

Piaget, J (1959) *The Construction of Reality in the Child.* New York: Basic Books.

Pointer, B (1993) *Movement Activities for Children with Learning Difficulties.* London: Jessica Kingsley.

Pointer, B (1995) '*Adapting movement activities for children with profound and multiple learning difficulties*', *British Journal of Physical Education,* vol 26, no 1, 28–30.

Sherborne, V (1990) *Developmental Movement for Children.* Cambridge: Cambridge University Press.

SCAA (1996a) *Desirable Outcomes for Children's Learning on entering compulsory education.* London: SCAA.

SCAA (1996b) *Planning the Curriculum for Pupils with Profound and Multiple Learning Difficulties.* London: SCAA.

Shreeves, R (1979) *Children Dancing*. London: Ward Lock Educational.

Siddall, J (1985) *Dancepack: a Resource Pack for Teaching Dance in Schools*. Norwich: Norfolk Educational Press.

Slade, P (1977) *Natural Dance*. Sevenoaks: Hodder and Stoughton.

Staffordshire County Council (1985) *Dance Curriculum Guidelines, 5–18 years*. Stafford: Staffordshire County Council.

Thorneycroft, M (1991) 'Partners in Dance', *Special Children*, no 48, May 1991, 19–22.

Upton, G (1979) *Physical and Creative Activities for the Mentally Handicapped*. Cambridge: Cambridge University Press.

Vygotsky, L S (1978) *Mind in Society: the Development of Higher Psychological Processes*. Cambridge, Mass.: Harvard University Press.

Warren, B (ed) (1993) *Using the Creative Arts in Therapy*. London: Routledge.

Wheeler, S (1995) 'Drama and Relationship Play in Early Years Education', *Drama*, vol 4, no 1, 5–7.

Wills, P and Peter, M J (1996) *Music For All*. London: David Fulton.

Wood, D J, Bruner, J S and Roff, G (1976) 'The Role of Tutoring in Problem-solving', *Journal of Child Psychology and Psychiatry*, vol 17, 89–100.

Index